The Women They Left Behind

Stories from Grimsby's fishing families

Nick Triplow ~ Tina Bramhill ~ Jade Shepherd

The Women They Left Behind: researched, written and edited by Nick Triplow, Tina Bramhill and Jade Shepherd. Cover illustration by Jenny Coy. Book design and layout by Tina Bramhill. Published by Fathom Press in association with CPO Media.

ISBN: 978 -0-9555950-3-5

Website: www.mycpomedia.com

This book is dedicated to:

The memory of Dolly Hardie 1920 – 2008

The fishing families of Grimsby

CONTENTS

Foreword 5

1. Birth of an Industry 7

2. Courting 13

3. Trawlers in War: 1914-1918 18

4. Between the Wars 23

5. Trawlers in War: 1939-1945 29

6. Sailing Days 39

7. Post-War Years 43

8. Money Matters 47

9. Women's Work 53

10. Coping Alone 65

11. Landing Days 72

12. High Days and Holidays 82

13. The Women They Left Behind 89

14. The Cod Wars 98

15. The Writing on the Wall 108

16. Dolly Hardie and the Fight for Compensation 114

About the Authors 125

Acknowledgements 127

Bibliography 129

FOREWORD

I don't think anyone would argue that the job of a fisherman was probably the toughest job in the world. For over 130 years men and boys fished out of Grimsby working in the most dangerous, hazardous conditions in order to put fish on the plates of the British people. For decades the fishing community in Grimsby and Cleethorpes endured hardship and tragedy; thousands lost their lives at sea doing work, as well as minesweeping in two world wars, leaving behind widows, orphans, mothers, fathers, brothers and sisters. The community would never have survived had it not been for the tremendous support of the women. In many ways their lives were just as tough and it took a very special breed of person to take on the job.

Bertha Coates with Doreen and David, two of her seven children

Life for a fisherman's wife could be lonely and stressful. As a child, I didn't think it unusual that my dad didn't come home from work each night. We only saw him for a few hours every two or three weeks or so. It wasn't until I was an adult that I realised how difficult it must have been for my mother. She brought up seven children almost single handed; she was both mother and father to us all. She saw we had a good education; we were always clothed and well fed and she was there when we were ill or needed help and advice. I know she often went without things herself when times were hard which they often were. She also taught us to respect others as well as ourselves, she taught us discipline (never harshly), good manners, and always to give up a bus seat to an elder. Apart from bringing up a family she also worked as a braider, first at Cosalt's in Sixhills Street, and later at home when I was very young. But this was nothing unusual; thousands of other fishermen's wives were doing exactly the same thing and had done for decades. If the phrase 'multi-tasking' had existed, it would most certainly have applied to these women.

For my part I did my bit 'down dock' late in life when I worked at the Fishermen's Mission for almost four years in a voluntary capacity. The role women played in the fishing industry is a vital part in Grimsby's heritage, sadly the like of which will never be seen again. With little or no visible evidence left of what was a truly special time, it is so important that as much information as possible is made available to ensure future generations realise how important the fishing industry was to this town and its people. I hope this book will go some way towards achieving that. I feel very privileged to have been invited to write these few words, and proud also that with four generations of fishermen in my family, they, along with the thousands of others in the fishing industry really did make Grimsby 'Great'.

Doreen Tyson
2009

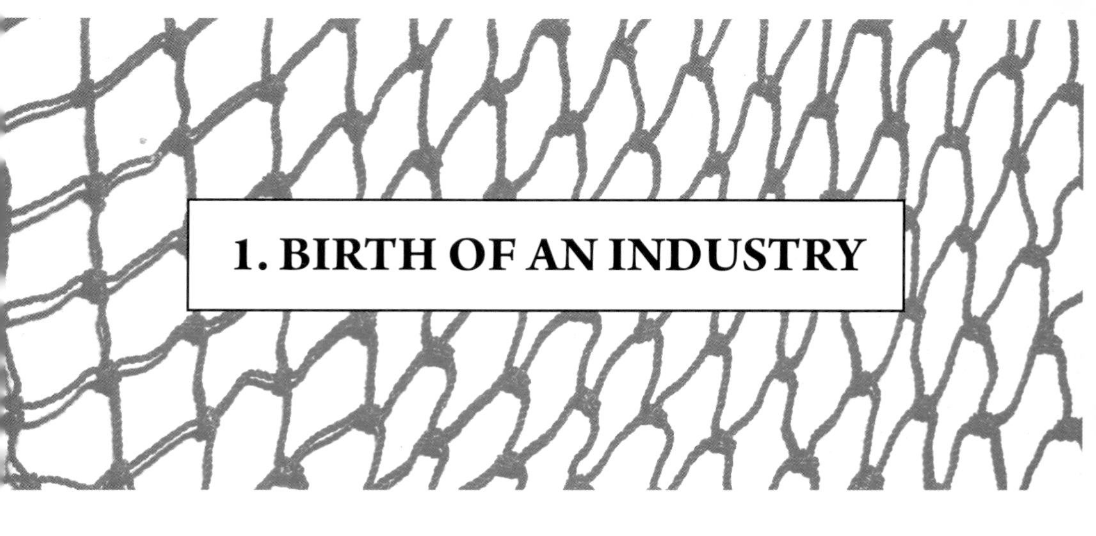

1. BIRTH OF AN INDUSTRY

'...you're going to Grimsby, you're gonna be a fisher boy.'

The first settlers landed in Grimsby from Scandinavia in AD 875. Legend has it that the town's Danish founder, Grim, lived by catching and selling fish with the help of his adopted son, Havelock. Certainly Grimsby's earliest settlers lived by fishing: records show that in the 11th century disputes arose between the abbots of Grimsby and the people of Lincoln over the price of tithes on fish. Documents dating back to the 14th and 15th century refer to large vessels venturing into the North Sea. Even in these earliest times fishing was an international affair, with regular trade recorded between Grimsby, Holland, Belgium, Norway and France.

At the end of the 18th century, Grimsby's population was less than 900. It remained isolated and generally unaffected by the Industrial Revolution until the 1840s. With the expansion of the railways across Britain, Grimsby was open to trade and there was interest in fishing from around the country. By 1848 Grimsby was thriving. Efforts to promote the town as a port were encouraged by the construction of the Royal Dock which began in 1846. Opening in 1852, the Royal Dock represented a turning point for Grimsby. Two towns emerged: the first, 'top town', was based around St. James's Church; the second, including Freeman Street and the dock area was two miles outside of the first. It was a bustling place thriving with immigrant workers who had helped build the dock and then stayed. Some of these were Irish labourers or Russian Jews on their way to America. Nearer to home, many had come to Grimsby from Suffolk, Yorkshire and Cumbria. In 1857

Grimsby's first fish dock opened. It covered six acres, was equipped with a floating pontoon which moved with the tide and enabled five vessels to unload their catch at any one time. From the second half of the 19th century, Grimsby's destiny became firmly linked with fishing to the virtual exclusion of all other industry.

The Pontoons on Grimsby Docks, Victorian era

In 1870 the Grimsby Co-operative Ice Company was formed and ice began to be shipped from Norway. The opening of a second fish dock in 1886 represented further development and transition. In 1890, to meet the growing fishing fleet's need for ice, an ice factory opened at the corner of Corporation Road and Victoria Street. As employment boomed, Grimsby took its place as one of Britain's greatest ports.

Working conditions for fishermen in the 19th century were deplorable. Once on board, the men often lived in squalor and faced incredible danger. Between 1884 - the first year records were kept - and 1894, over 2,000 men and boys were killed. This was mostly the result of 'fleeting', a system by which a number of ships would transfer their catch to one other ship to bring back to port. As well as being a hazardous undertaking in itself, this involved ships spending prolonged periods at sea.

As the industry grew, trawler owners were drawn to the system of apprenticeships to meet the increasing demand for labour. A large proportion of apprentices were found in workhouses and reformatories. By 1872 there were 1,350 boys in the industry compared to 1,150 trained men.

When a boy signed on he was effectively a prisoner. Conditions at sea were filthy and records indicate that large numbers of boys died or were seriously injured. The apprenticeship system began to attract criticism. By 1871, the Local Government Board had received numerous complaints that a large number of boys apprenticed to the fishing trade in Grimsby had either been sent to prison or run away because of the poor conditions. Owners were prepared to punish boys unwilling to serve and force them to return to their duties and, if necessary, send them to prison. Charles Brocklesby was a young apprentice charged with refusing to go to sea. He was sentenced to one month in prison with hard labour in 1860. He was by no means alone; between 29 September 1876 and 29 September 1877 there were 261 cases of apprentices being committed with an average sentence length of 22½ days.

It is hardly surprising that boys were reluctant to go to sea. Newspapers were filled with stories of the cruelty to which they were subjected. In Grimsby some owners were brought before the courts on charges of assault. The Board of Guardians appointed Baldwyn Fleming, member of the Royal Commission on Pauperism, to inquire into the allegations. Fleming found no evidence that apprentices were badly treated. However, letters continued to circulate regarding cases of assault and ill treatment of apprentices at sea. In 1878 another inquiry was held, this time led by Messrs. Allen Stoneham and George J Swanston.

Like Fleming, Stoneham and Swanston were broadly supportive of the apprenticeship system, but they did condemn a lack of supervision and made a number of recommendations which the Board of Trade implemented almost immediately. In 1880 the Grimsby Superintendent began to keep details of apprentices. A record was opened when a boy signed his agreement. It recorded his name, age, place of origin, period of service, name of master, and where he was to live. Fleming noted that there were two types of apprentice - indoor and outdoor. The former 'lived-in' and received food and clothing from their masters; the latter were paid a weekly wage, varying between seven and 16 shillings, from which they paid for lodgings and keep while ashore. There was, he said, a need for training and moral education. He proposed control over pubs and brothels, regular inspection of vessels, reports on the character of masters, regular visits to the port by representatives of The Board of Guardians and trial trips to assess each boy's suitability for fishing.

Despite the implementation of certain recommendations, outcry over the system continued with the controversy reaching Parliament. In 1882, President of the Board of Trade Joseph Chamberlain appointed an inquiry committee. This recommended that no boy under the age of 16 should be employed on larger vessels, that each should have one month's trial and if found unsuitable, he should be returned to his home or institution. No boy under the age of 13 should be considered. By this time, however, some of the problems had been remedied by the 1880 Merchant Shipping Act which removed the threat of immediate arrest at the whim of the owners and also imprisonment for desertion. By 1915, the number of apprentices had reduced significantly and the system disappeared altogether in 1929.

Mike Connor's grandfather was one of those for whom a life at sea was a decision made on his behalf, making him a 'conscript' to the industry.

> 'Me Granddad Swan was actually an orphan. It's not known this, he was from Cambridge. And the people who run the orphanage went to him one day and said, "...you're going to Grimsby, you're gonna be a fisher boy." He said, "I've never heard of Grimsby. What's that?" The orphanage used to sell boys to trawler owners – modern day slavery it was. But he was a tough old stick and he worked his way up to be a skipper.'

The first trade unions began to appear in the port towards the end of the 19th century. In 1897 the Grimsby Steam Fishing Vessels and Engineers and Fireman's Union was established although, because of the nature of the industry - primarily the difficulty of ensuring large numbers of fishermen to facilitate mass action - it was always difficult to organise union protest effectively.

However, the first year of the 20th century was marked with a strike on Grimsby's dock. On 1 July 1901 the Grimsby Steam Fishing Vessels Engineers and Firemen's Union and the National Sailors and Firemen's Union told trawler owners that unless improved offers of pay were made, they would refuse to sail. The owners' response was to tie up their ships and tell the fishermen to drop their demands or go without work. In spite of a marginally improved offer from the owners, the dispute worsened. By September, there were signs of starvation among fishermen's families. Free breakfasts were provided for the destitute; concerts were held to raise money to feed children; and local timber merchant Sam Ellis threw a huge party for 3,000 children in Grimsby's People's Park. In the London newspapers, appeals were made for food and help.

Steam trawlers laid up during the 1901 strike, Grimsby

On 19 September, after 81 days on strike, militant fishermen gathered at the federation offices. Owners fled as the men smashed windows and destroyed the premises. The mood of fishermen hardened and large scale union meetings were held. Freeman Street was the scene of huge rallies which were supported by sympathetic unionists from Hull and Leeds. Union leaders tried to pacify the mob but they failed. When Chief Constable Stirling arrived he was stoned and later remarked that, 'Smashing windows...will not feed empty bellies.' Stirling contacted the Sheffield police who dispatched an additional 85 police officers. As night came the situation remained volatile, and another call was made, this time to Lincoln. Soldiers from the Lincolnshire Regiment were immediately sent to Grimsby. The following day the Riot Act was read in Riby Square initiating a return to relative calm. Ironically, the only major damage had been to Sam Ellis's timber yard which was set on fire. On 6 October both parties agreed to a settlement brokered by Lords Yarborough and Heneage. The following day 55 trawlers sailed from Grimsby. The lock-out was over.

In spite of the hardships and poor pay; working conditions that were at best tough and at worst lethal, the traditions of Grimsby as a fishing town were well established by the beginning of the 20th century. Doreen Tyson has traced her fishing family's origins back to the heyday of Grimsby as a booming Victorian town.

> 'I never knew my great grandfather. He was one of four brothers who came over from Manchester to be a fishing apprentice in the 1880s. Of these four brothers, two stayed in Grimsby and two went to fish in Hull. I think they came over looking for work because during the American Civil War, there was no cotton going into Manchester. And if you look in any of the censuses for Grimsby hardly anybody was born in Grimsby from 1860 onwards - they were coming from all over the country; apprentices from the workhouses and the orphanages were coming and working here. They came looking for work, and Grimsby was booming.
>
> 'My grandfather was a fisherman as well. When he'd stopped fishing I got to know him. He got his allotment and he used to come down and visit us with his produce. Then there was my dad and the only other one in the family was my brother and he went fishing so I've had four generations of fishermen in the family.'

Migration to Grimsby in early days of the boom didn't only come from the urban heartlands of the industrial revolution. Joan Harrison's family history points to migration from further afield, fishermen encouraged by the promise of work.

> 'My father's ancestors came from Beer in Devon. They were fishermen and they came up here to Grimsby in the 1840s. They went back a few years later, but the great great grandson stayed here and he started a family in Grimsby.'

Mike Connor's paternal grandfather had a difficult journey to Grimsby, overcoming obstacles to find work in the industry.

> 'Me Grandfather Connor, he lived in Scarborough and in 1928 there was no ships there. Nobody would lend him the money so he actually walked to Grimsby. He walked round through Goole. He actually walked, there was no point thumbing it, there was no cars on the road. He got a house down Brereton Avenue, and then he sent for my granny and the six kids. And me dad was one of those six kids, he was eight year old and that's how he came round this area. All my family got here in various ways through the fishing industry. It was a thriving town. Even in 1928 when me grandfather came it was thriving, there was ships here and the trawler owners were already very wealthy people.'

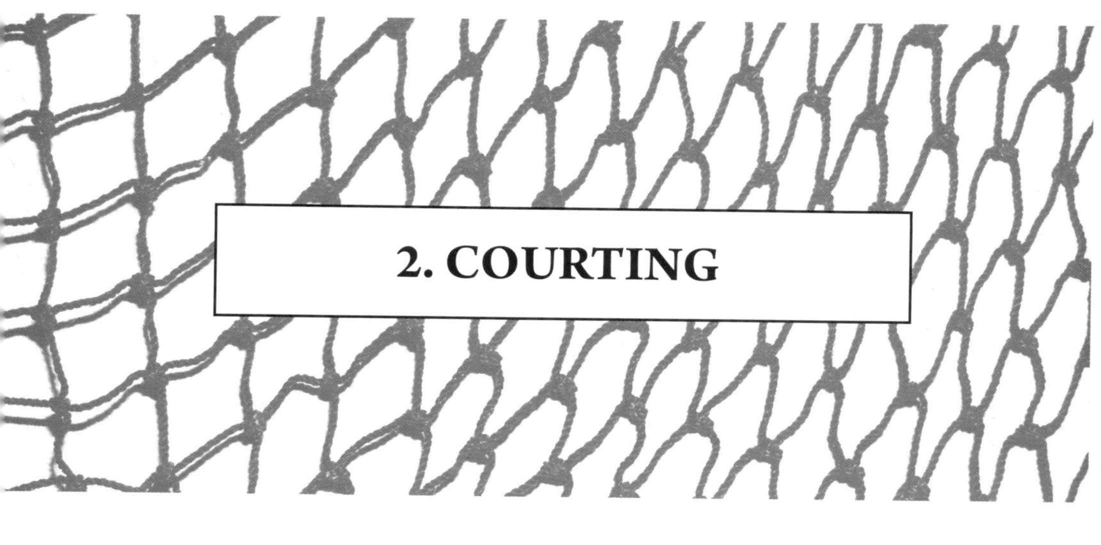

2. COURTING

'I told my daughter, don't marry a fisherman.'

For every young woman who met, courted and married a fisherman, there is a story of life lived apart. The vast majority of fishermen's wives coped alone with the duties of mother and father, dealing with daily hardships, uncertainty about money and the dangers her husband faced at sea. It helped, of course, if you'd come from the fishing tradition and could call on an extended family for support, but even knowing what you were letting yourself in for didn't always prevent the early days of a marriage from being a difficult time.

Olga Drever married Steve on 26 December 1947. She was 20 years old. He was 19 and had been a fisherman for two years.

> 'I didn't like being married to a fisherman at first. All the time you were worrying, fed up at being on your own, because you were still young and you wanted to go out. Course, when they came in you had a ball if they'd had a good trip, and he was pretty lucky, Steve – he was on some decent ships. I worked in a pub, then in a shop, just part

Olga and Steve Drever

-time when the kids were small. I used to love being a fisherman's wife. My sister, she was married to a civvy, and she used to say she was jealous of me being married to a fisherman because they'd got all the money, but they didn't, not every time. It was just luck if they got on a good ship, a good and happy ship that was the main thing.'

Rita Whittle hadn't come from a fishing family, but the realities of life as a fisherman's wife were soon evident when, for the first few months of her marriage to George - a deep sea fisherman - he was away from anything between 22 days and six weeks at a time. If Rita's mum had had her way, the wedding might not have taken place at all.

> 'When we were courting he'd come to meet me at the house and he'd be three parts drunk. I remember the week before I was getting married my mum was going to come up the church and stop the wedding because of the drink. I thought I could change him. You do, when you're daft and young.
>
> 'We got married in 1953 on the day after my twentieth birthday. Things were rationed so we had to cut down at the wedding reception and they saved up all their coupons to get me a pair of woollen blankets. My mother wouldn't let me live at home when I was married, it wasn't right, so we went into rooms and I carried on doing shop work. We were married three months and I fell pregnant with my eldest. She was born the following March when he was at sea. I had four kids and my husband was away when two of them were born. They had a father, but we were a one parent family for most of the time. I had some good times and some bad times. I made my bed and I had to lie on it, but it was a different era. I told my daughter, don't marry a fisherman.'

Emma Brennan's father had been a fisherman, but that hadn't prepared her for the first time she met Dennis.

> 'He was an utter disgrace. He fell out of a taxi! So we won't go any further - he'd been "on the pop" with my brother at that young age – sixteen or seventeen. So me mother said, "Bring 'em both in, put 'em both on the settee and they'll sleep it off." So that's what we did. I looked at him and I didn't really like him. I didn't get on with him - I'd seen the state he was in. My mother was a strict Catholic, she wouldn't allow that for girls, but she knew the lads had a drink. He used to bring me a little gift, or a tin

of salmon for me mother. He knew I smoked so he'd bring me a pack of cigarettes. Well I never had a lot of money. I had about half a crown left when I was finished paying me lodgings and bills. And he said, "Do you want to go out?" And I thought to myself, *well I haven't got any money*. "Yeah, yeah, I'll go out with yer." And that was it – we took it from there. We went to the Palace Buffet and the theatre; Dorothy Squires was on. And I used to like to hear her singing and I thought, *oh this is gonna be lovely*. And where did we get stuck? You know you used to have these poles, and I had to look round. So that put me off again. I went, "Is this the best seat you could get?" And he said, "Well, it was the last two." Anyway, we left it at that and walked home over the footbridge because you weren't allowed out late at night. About ten o'clock if we were stood in the doorway doing a bit of talking or kissing, me mother or father'd shout, "C'mon!" And you went in.

'We kept going out with each other and we were sat on the doorstep one day and he said, "Will you marry me?" So I said I'd think about it. Eventually I said to me mother, "Do you think I should?" She said, "Yeah he's a good man, a good worker. You'll not want." So I married him in St Luke's Church on Heneage Road.'

The first few weeks of Ann Graves' marriage to Graham brought to light some domestic problems. If Graham thought Ann was an easy touch, she soon straightened things out.

'He come flying down the stairs and said, "You haven't ironed me socks! My mother always irons my socks." I told him to take 'em round to his flipping mother then, I'd never ironed a sock in my life. So he said he'd do it himself. "Well do it," I said. He had to have his socks ironed. And every time he went off to sea he'd say, "Take my suits to the cleaners won't yer?" Now for the first year, maybe eighteen months, I did. He might have only worn a suit once for a dinner when we'd gone out, but it had to be cleaned. I don't remember what it cost then, but I thought, *it's better off in my purse than it is in theirs*. So what I started to do whenever he took the suit off and just threw it, I picked it up, hung it up and I used to save the ticket and plastic that it come covered in from the cleaners so I'd stick it back on. He used to say, "How much do I owe you for cleaning?" And I'd tell him, "You don't owe me, you owe my mother." So he used to give my mother the money. She used to say, "Oh I feel awful." I'd tell her to just shove it her purse until he'd gone away. Otherwise, I'd never have had any money when he wasn't there.'

Marjorie Louis met George when he was a 17 year old galley boy, although at first he wasn't entirely truthful about his age.

> 'He told me he was eighteen – fibber! Cause we met in the pub! And then he took his second cook and baker's ticket at the college for fishermen on Lockhill Corner. And I had to pay for the pictures and buy his fags, because his mother wanted the money that he got for his lodge. Money was tight wasn't it, and she didn't keep him for nothing. When he got his ticket, he went in the Merchant Navy. He went in I would say for two or three years and he was missing me, bless him. He came home and we got engaged in 1952. We'd been courting two years. We got married in 1954. From then on it was twelve months later, and there she was! Bless her. Then thirteen months after that there was another one. And this was what they did. Every time they came in dock a baby was conceived. So four, that's how many babies I had in four and a half years.'

When Janet Cox first met her husband Keith, one of the few remaining Grimsby fishermen, he was taking some time away from the sea. It soon became clear that his time ashore was coming to an end.

> 'I met him when he was seventeen and I was fifteen. He was working on the land, but he'd already been to sea. It was just like he was having a break really. I soon realised that it was what he was going to do for the rest of his life. His dad took him as soon as he left school. Everyone said he was a fantastic footballer and that's what he should have done, but they came for him after he'd gone to sea so that was the end of that.'

They married in 1966. For the first year, they lived with Janet's parents before buying their first home, a detached bungalow in the relatively prosperous area of Humberston.

> 'That's how good the fishing industry was then. Most of them in Humberston were older then us. I went to my mother's a lot. Well I had a child by the time we got a place. I had a child while he was away. Births, deaths, marriages, hospital, anything – they'd just miss it all. If you sent a message they might get it within a week. He didn't find out when I had me son till he was about a week old. You would tell the office and they

would wire it via telegraph or telegram. We had four children in the end and I stayed at home until the eldest one was sixteen. I think the first few years we were married I hoped he'd come out of it, then I realised he wouldn't. It was all he'd ever known.'

3. TRAWLERS IN WAR: 1914-1918

'Heroes who sail the mine-strewn seas'

Grimsby's fishermen performed a vital and costly role during both world wars, turning their skills to the new and dangerous task of clearing Britain's coasts and shipping lanes of enemy mines as well as continuing to catch fish to feed the nation. The Grimsby fleet lost 419 trawlers during both wars, the vast majority due to enemy action.

Grimsby's role in the development of trawlers as minesweepers can be traced back to Admiral Lord Charles Beresford's visit to the town in 1907. Beresford requested a demonstration of trawling methods. Two trawlers - *Andes* and *Algoma,* were engaged for the trials. Dummy mines were placed and the trawlers instructed to sweep them; a task they successfully completed. Beresford was impressed, clearly there was potential for trawler use in minesweeping and the trials led to an agreement with Grimsby trawler owners to form a reserve in the event of conflict.

In 1914, 156 Grimsby trawlers were contracted to serve as minesweepers. However, this proved to be inadequate preparation and when war broke out the industry was largely unprepared. Large numbers of fishermen were called up for service as members of the Royal Naval Reserve, others to crew reserved trawlers. Of the 700 steam trawlers in the port, 600 were requisitioned and manned by some 6,000 volunteers.

As news of the declaration of war spread, trawler skippers navigated back to port. Within a month, over 200 trawlers were laying idle in the dock. Only No. 1 Fish Dock was used for the landing of fish.

At noon on 8 August 1914, fishermen along the East Coast were mobilised and formed the National Auxiliary Patrol. Two days later it was reported that the channel had been swept clear of mines. The first Auxiliary Patrol consisted of 50 steam drifters manned by 500 fishermen enrolled as members of the Royal Naval Reserve. Nobody was prepared for what was to follow as many Grimsby fishermen, carried on the patriotic fervour of the early days of the war, signed up for service with the Trawler Reserve.

Wartime fishing was a highly dangerous task. In addition to the usual peacetime dangers, trawlers were subject to enemy attack. The threat of mines on the North Sea was so severe that no fishing crew member was obligated to go to sea. All crew members who left the dock did so as volunteers.

On 7 September 1914, the *Grimsby Telegraph* printed the names of Grimsby trawlers already sunk by the Germans, these were the *Argonaut*; *Lobelia*; *Harrier*; *Fortunia*; *Chameleon*; *Pegasus*; *Pollux*; *Rideo*; *Rhine*; *Seti*; and *Valiant*. The Grimsby trawler *Kilmarnock* lost six crew members when the trawler, owned by Consolidated Fisheries Ltd., struck a mine. Leaving Grimsby on 22 September 1914, *Kilmarnock* was on its way to the North Sea fishing lanes when the skipper noticed two mines and ordered a buoy to be placed over them intending to return to Grimsby to report the matter. However, he sighted a naval vessel and altered his course with the purpose of informing its crew of the mines. There was an explosion and the *Kilmarnock* broke in half and sunk almost immediately. The *Raboao* sank in the same position as the *Kilmarnock* on 24 September. This time loss of life was not so severe, nevertheless, the third hand was reported missing. Other trawler losses included the *Acantha* in 1915 - torpedoed whilst fishing in the North Sea, and the *Zarina, Vanilla,* and *Recolo* the same year. *Zarina* and *Vanilla* were attacked by German submarines whilst fishing, and it was reported that *Recolo* was either attacked by the Germans or hit a mine.

On 4 May 1915, seven fishing vessels (six from Hull, one from Grimsby) were sunk in a submarine attack. The submarine surfaced 100 yards away from Grimsby trawler *Collingwood* and signalled the crew to stop the engines, abandon ship and board their lifeboat. The trawling gear had just come aboard and the submarine was clearly visible. After a brief discussion, the crew decided that the odds were against the trawler and decided to make a run for it. As the *Collingwood* steamed away

Zarina (right) lost in 1915

the submarine chased her, firing numerous shots, causing the men on deck to run for cover. The chase lasted for no more than a quarter of an hour. The only explanation the crew could give as to why the submarine allowed the *Collingwood* to escape was that the Grimsby trawler *Rugby*, fishing nearby, had her trawl down and was an easier target. The judgement was borne out as *Collingwood's* crew witnessed the *Rugby* explode.

At the annual meeting of the Grimsby Unionist Association on 26 February 1915, the role Grimsby's men and trawlers played in the war as minesweepers was commended. Concerns were also expressed at the profound effect on the fishing trade of the employment of Grimsby's fishermen and trawlers in war work with trawler owners complaining that too many boats had been requisitioned.

The heroism of Grimsby's minesweepers was recognised nationally with the *Pall Mall Gazette* referring to fishermen as, '...heroes who sail the mine-strewn seas' and praising their 'nerves of steel'. The response of Grimsby's fishermen was typically understated. They said, simply, 'You get used to it.'

While the war continued, restrictions were placed on fishing grounds and a limit placed on the number of vessels passing in and out of port. Consequently, there was a drastic decline in fish supplies. The knock-on effect of this for the men involved in buying, selling, handling and packing of fish was considerable. The war increased insurance premiums. This meant higher wages and running expenses, which escalated the price of fish. Grimsby's economy was hit hard by the war since it had no other large industry to support it. While it was true that the number of men committed to the minesweepers ensured no fishermen need be out of work, those employed in allied trades on land were less fortunate. Fitters, net-braiders, and fish house workers suffered as a result.

Although the most dangerous years of the war were the earliest - it was publicly acknowledged in May 1915 that Grimsby had suffered significantly with 40 vessels blown up by mines, resulting in the deaths of around 300 men - losses continued throughout. Men fishing faced the same threats from mines and enemy craft as the men working on the minesweepers, and they received increased insurance premiums and war risk money as an addition to their wages.

The number of men losing their lives while fishing was so alarming that the Fishermen's Emergency Relief Fund was established to provide relief for widows and families of fishermen lost as a result of enemy action. Such dangers led to concerns in 1915 that unless the Government acted, Grimsby would have to stop fishing altogether. The fear of going to sea unprotected with the constant threat of a submarine attack meant it had become difficult to secure the men to continue fishing. In June 1915, the lack of protection led four Grimsby trawlers to form a pact. The skippers of the *Andes, Grimenco, Rodrigo,* and *Alexandra* arranged to fish in each others company. It was agreed that if any of them caught sight of a German submarine, they would assemble by a pre-arranged signal. If any ship came under attack, the others would engage the enemy from different angles. On 11 June, the *Grimenco* sighted an enemy submarine three miles away. The skipper signalled a warning to the three other trawlers. They steamed together and awaited action. The submarine surfaced and was reportedly surprised at the manoeuvre which resulted in it seeing a trawler at every angle ready to advance. The stand off lasted some time. It appeared that the Germans did not know how to react since the actions of the trawlers made it impossible for her to move closer. As night fell, the trawlers separated and made their way safely to port.

The perils of fishing during the war extended to the threat of being taken prisoner. The *Virgilia* left Grimsby for the Faroe fishing grounds on 24 May and was returning on 3 June when she was attacked by a German submarine off the Scottish coast. The attack began at midnight and although none of the shots fired from the submarine hit the trawler, the crew abandoned ship. They boarded a small boat, but were overhauled by

The trawler *Andes* - formed a pact with three other trawlers

the submarine. The fishermen were made to stand on the submarine's foredeck, while the skipper, Rawlins, was ordered to remain in the conning tower as the Germans placed bombs aboard the *Virgilia* and then helped themselves to some fish. *Virgilia's* crew were allowed to make their own way to shore in the lifeboat and Rawlins was informed that he was a prisoner. The submarine's commander asked questions about England's food supply: *how long could she last*? To which Rawlins replied, 'ten years'. The following night, off the north-east coast near Hartlepool, the submarine's gunner, who Rawlins had befriended, informed him they were preparing for action. At 10 o'clock a ship was spotted. The submarine surfaced and opened fire. However, the patrol vessel had superior firepower and the counter-attack was so severe that the crew aboard the submarine believed it was the end. After they made their escape, Rawlins was confined to the engine room and did not see daylight for eight days. During his time aboard, he was present for the torpedoing of five steamers. Eight days later, he was put ashore at Heligoland.

In 1918 when hostilities ended, 298 Grimsby trawlers, either fishing or engaged in war work, had been lost at sea with the loss of 398 men.

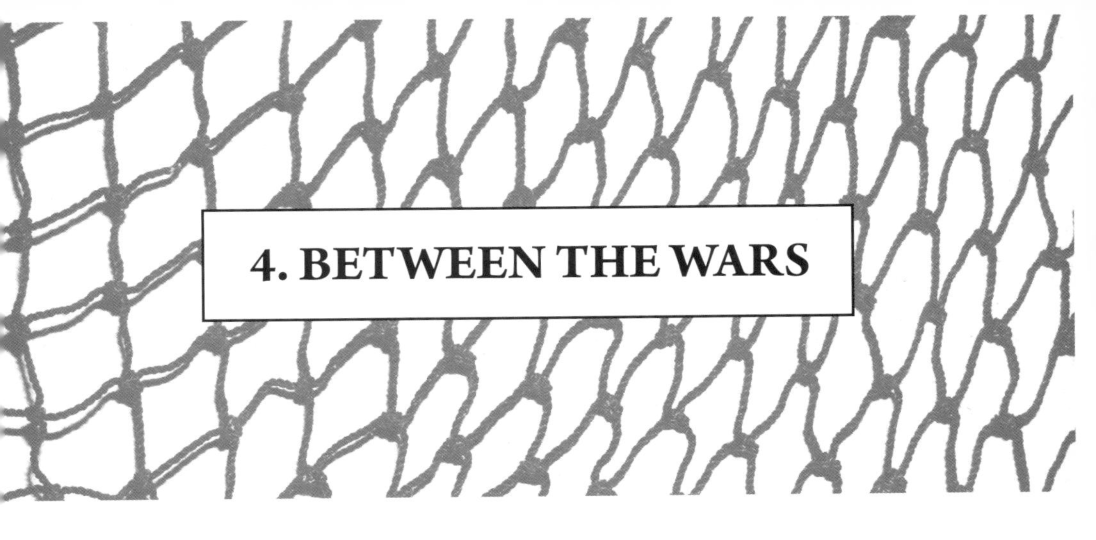

4. BETWEEN THE WARS

'Freeman Street was a gold mine.'

After the First World War, the priority for the fishing industry was re-converting Admiralty-requisitioned trawlers back into fishing vessels. New trawlers were commissioned to replace those lost. Predictably, since this would take time, owners preferred to acquire previously requisitioned vessels to make the most of replenished fish stocks – the result of four years of enforced conservation.

While the conditions endured by fishermen in the immediate post-war period remained much as they had pre-1914, there were developments from outside the industry. However, in contrast with the development of trade unions in other industries, fishing unions remained relatively weak throughout the 1920s and 1930s. In 1917 a retired Grimsby skipper, Captain Bingham, had established the National Union of British Fishermen which, by the end of 1919, had a membership of 51,000 men based primarily at the Humber ports. At the end of the war attempts were made to spread unionisation and disputes broke out. Fishermen's cases were undermined by the lack of union traditions, inter-union disputes and factional interests. Conversely, employers had developed strong associations in many ports and in 1919 the British Trawler Federation was established to oversee their interests nationally. When, in January 1919, Grimsby trawler crews went on strike, it was not a union backed action but the result of a grass roots demand for improved wages.

In February 1921, Government wartime price controls were lifted. Owners

Freeman Street, 1930s

immediately cut labour costs. In April a revised scale of wages saw the abolition of 'trip money' for skippers and mates in the three largest ports (Hull, Grimsby and Fleetwood). The six shilling sea bonus for deckhands disappeared and was replaced by an extra penny in the pound share money. As a result, many groups of workers faced wage cuts as profits fell and unemployment increased in the early 1920s. Fishermen drifted away from unions. The National Union of British Fishermen ceased to exist in its own right when, in 1922, it amalgamated with the Transport and General Workers Union (TGWU).

The Easter landings of 1926 set a post-war record, and the numbers of vessels arriving in dock was so great that 59 were unable to land. Those waiting in the Humber had to wait two tides and landed a day late.

Annie Bell worked in a series of pubs near the docks in the 1930s.

> 'Freeman Street was a gold mine. When the Icelanders come they used to take pianos back on the ship, washing machines, wirelesses, and clothes for their wives. The Danes come over and them poor buggers had nowt at the beginning, I mean they only went on seine netters as deckies and that. Some became top skippers earning the best money going, but they never forgot people that were good to them. One of 'em come in the Lincoln Arms one day and he says, "Anna, you remember when I first came over here, I sat in the blue room there didn't I? I had no money and I asked you to trust me until I see my friends didn't I?" I said, "Well yeah, that was only a ten shilling note." He said, "I've got something for you." So he called the gaffer, Mr Stillings, and he said, "This girl I give her this." It was a white fiver. I said I couldn't take it and he said, "Yes Anna, you were the only friend that was good for me that day. You have small ones, buy them something, take them to Cleethorpes." A white fiver in them days, I thought I was a millionaire.'

By the 1930s the British Trawler Federation represented most owners, although ports tended to retain their own associations. For fishermen, disputes over stocker-bait money, cod liver oil money, and poundage share affected all crew members, increasing the divisions among them. Men felt that corruption was widespread, but had little chance of preventing it. Fishing and trawling remained highly hazardous and the absence of union influence was instrumental in the lack of improvement in pay and conditions.

In 1930, a Board of Trade edict made it compulsory for all trawlers to carry a wireless and an operator, which until then had been regarded a luxury. Consequently trawlers were able to fish further afield and there was a need for larger ships. Of the 88 new trawlers registered in the 1930s, 35 were the new, larger vessels at least 140 feet long. By the end of the decade there were 600 trawlers using the port which itself had expanded once more. Lord Farringdon cut the first sod of the construction of a new fish dock. Fish Dock No. 3 opened on 4 October 1934, providing more water and space for the fleet of larger vessels. The opening was a grand local event. A marquee for 700 guests was erected and the Consolidated Fisheries' new trawler *Grimsby Town* made the momentous journey to the new dock.

Grimsby Town entering the new dock

The Grimsby Mission and Rosina Ada Newnham MBE

In the years immediately after the First World War, the Grimsby mission came into its own. As a Christian charity it had provided financial, practical and spiritual help to fishermen and their families since the latter part of the 19th century. In May 1895, Captain Smedley was appointed Port Missioner for Grimsby. He was

Rosina Ada Newnham

instrumental in opening a mission at Cleethorpes, initially over a fish shop, where visitors reported, '...the smell pervaded the premises throughout the week, with a stale odour lingering during Sunday services.'

In 1899, a hostel was established in Riby Square. An anonymous donor had provided the town with money to build a facility for unemployed fishermen, many of whom came to Grimsby looking for work and had no money or lodgings. The mission fed many during the strike of 1901 and, in 1904, moved to a building on the corner of Tiverton Street and Harrington Street.

The mission also welcomed a new and formidable superintendent in 1904. Born in Portsmouth on 20 January 1866, Rosina Ada Newnham began what was to be a lifelong commitment to the well-being of mariners in 1891. Beginning as a visitor at the Sailor's Rest at Stoke Damerel, Devon, in 1901 she became an officer at the Sailor's Rest in Devonport.

In 1904, she was appointed Superintendent of the Royal National Mission to Deep Sea Fishermen (RNMDSF) at Grimsby. On arrival, she lived in a house in Orwell Street which was later to become part of the mission premises. Miss Newnham was to see the mission develop alongside the industry for the next 30 years.

Even before the outbreak of the First World War it was clear that the mission was inadequate to meet the demands of the growing industry and its community. Plans for a new building were developed, but these were shelved at the outbreak of war.

Within three months of the declaration of war, 20 Grimsby vessels had been destroyed, 83 men were lost and 128 were known to be prisoners. As he would throughout the war, Captain Smedley had the unenviable duty of delivering the news to countless families that their loved ones had perished.

Miss Newnham remained committed to her work of helping fishermen and their families. She made a request through the mission journal Toilers of the Deep, for, 'black dresses, jackets, stockings, anything in the way of mourning garments for the widows and orphans of the men who have perished.' A distress fund was also established for widows. Under the direction of Miss Newnham the RNMDSF made the care of the fishermen prisoners its war work.

The Royal National Mission to Deep Sea Fishermen in Grimsby, under Miss Newnham's direction, sent out 33,909 food parcels to prisoners of war along with 1,697 parcels of boots and clothing. A total of £1,049,17s, 6d was spent on relief work with a large proportion of the money coming from the South Adelaide Fund. Simultaneously, the mission helped war widows and wives, and knitting work was provided. The women knitted a total of 7,255 pairs of sea boot stockings, 605 pairs of socks, 33 jerseys, and 26 pairs of meltor twine gloves, all of which were sent to aid the fishermen.

When the fishing trade entered a slump immediately after the First World War, the Mission remained fully occupied supporting fishermen and families. The pre-war scheme for a new build was revived and the hostel in Cleethorpe Road was turned into temporary headquarters while the new building was prepared.

Built at a cost of £20,000, The Queen Mary Hostel was opened by Princess Mary on April 23, 1925. Newspapers reported the hostel as being, '...advanced enough to show how a fine feature of the town it will be, and how well adapted to the lives of our deep-sea fishermen.'

The mission's growth under Miss Newnham was enormous. The work she undertook showed dedication and compassion in regard to the plight of fishermen and their families. Yet she remained modest about her work. In an interview she gave to the *Grimsby News* in March 1935 she was too busy to provide a photograph for the article, saying, 'Just put in a photo of the hostel instead, the readers will be more interested in that.'

The Queen Mary Hostel

The story of Miss

Newnham's life is the story of the Grimsby mission's early years. Her aim was to make it a home away from home for the fishermen who had travelled to Grimsby and to make the lives of fishermen who resided in the town as comfortable as possible and care for their families in times of need. The work Miss Newnham did as superintendent was appreciated and acknowledged by fishermen and the fishing community as this letter from a former resident shows.

> 'Dear Friend, I now take the great pleasure of writing these few lines to thank you for your great kindness towards me while I was stopping at Grimsby at the RNMDSF Hostel. It gives me a joyful heart when I think of the kindness that you and your staff bestowed on me while I was at Grimsby...'

On her retirement from the mission in June 1936, Mr Hymus Jones presented Miss Newnham with a bound Bible on behalf of the men who attended the Sunday afternoon meetings. She also received an oak granddaughter clock on behalf of the staff and friends of the hostel and was presented with a fitted wardrobe at the weekly meeting of the wives and fishermen. The Mayor and Council of the Borough of Grimsby presented her with a bouquet and a handbag and purse containing a cheque for £60. In June 1936 it was announced that Miss Newnham was to be awarded an MBE.

Miss Newnham died in Grimsby on 18 June 1962 at the age of 96, and was buried in Scartho Road Cemetery.

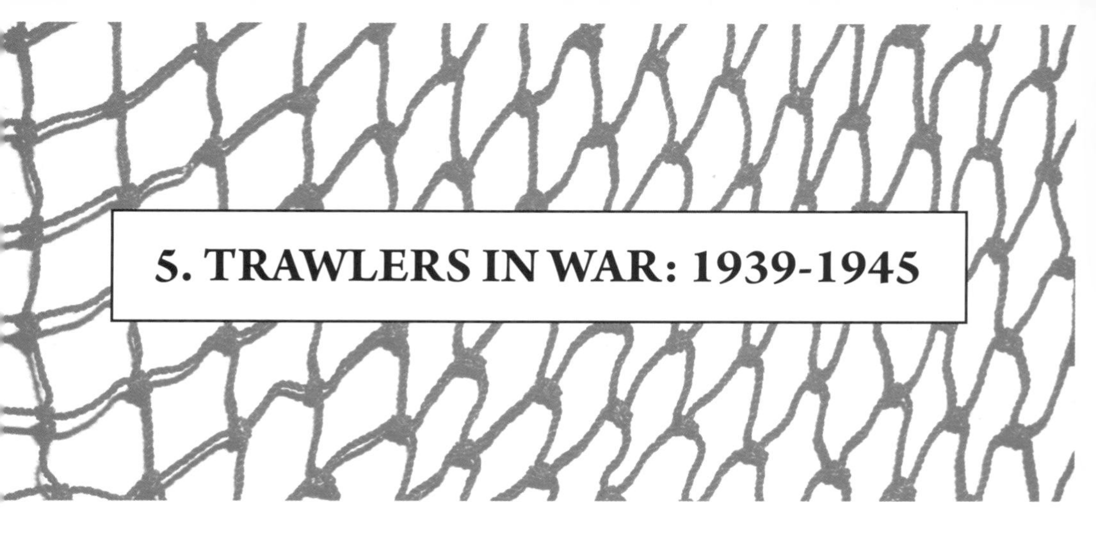

5. TRAWLERS IN WAR: 1939-1945

'A significant proportion of our whole war effort had to be devoted to combating the mine...'

Grimsby's fishing fleet fought on two fronts throughout the Second World War. Some vessels continued to fish as others were requisitioned for service with the Royal Navy as minesweepers and auxiliary patrol vessels. The Government was determined to be well prepared and as early as 1938, ships began to be requisitioned as they returned from the fishing grounds. Article nine of the Naval Treaties prohibited the transformation of trawlers into armed vessels during times of peace, so the ships were requisitioned or commissioned as vessels of war prior to arming them.

Before the outbreak of war the Royal Navy had 40 minesweepers in service. Half of these were coal-burning sweepers launched during the previous war known as 'Smokey Joes'. At the wartime peak, there were more than 1,000 British minesweepers in action, a large number manned by fishermen, many from the Grimsby fleet. In the four weeks prior to the outbreak of war, 250 Grimsby trawlers were bought or requisitioned by the Admiralty.

Trawlers were fitted with Oropesa Sweeps – as were the Navy's fleet minesweepers - which towed under water and cut mine cables, allowing them to float to the surface and be destroyed. Trawlers were armed with guns, depth charge throwers and chutes. Hulls were strengthened to support the weight of the extra armament, and additional fresh water tanks installed.

As war became a certainty, work began in Grimsby on the conversion of trawlers *Dalmatia, Waveflower,* and *Crestflower*. These were to be manned by the R.N.R Patrol Service personnel recruited from volunteer fishermen. The Admiralty retained around 300 men for service in the Royal Navy trawlers.

The outbreak of war brought mixed feelings for the 12 year old Margaret Monger. Her father had been at sea when war was declared. When his ship was requisitioned he joined up.

> 'He needn't have done – he was thirty-six by this time, but he went in the Navy as skipper of a minesweeper. Fortunately, he was based here in Grimsby so we probably saw more of him in that five years than in the previous twelve.'

Margaret's father continued to skipper minesweepers throughout the war and was awarded the Distinguished Service Cross on 22 December 1942 in recognition of: 'Courage, endurance and devotion to duty in Minesweeping operations.' In wartime as in peacetime, John Calver Monger was reluctant to talk about what went on at sea, refusing to discuss the action that led to the decoration.

> 'If you got the DSO you were the leader of a combined effort, but the DSC was for personal bravery - he never said what for. They used to sweep the North Sea and I do know that one time the boats both sides of him were blown up, but that was war. Most of the ships were trawlers in Grimsby. I know the first one was a little drifter minesweeper, *The Red Sky*.
>
> 'When he received his DSC from the King in 1943, we went to the Palace with him, mum and me. We didn't go into the normal room they use for that sort of thing; we went into the Long Room. We went down to London and stayed overnight and came back the next day. Of course by then he was in the Navy.'

Margaret's father was to be decorated a second time, receiving an MBE from the Queen for work on the Ernest Holt expeditionary vessel in 1956. On this occasion Margaret's sister made the trip to Buckingham Palace.

Once requisitioned, a trawler's peacetime skipper was officially placed in command. Some had been trained in the Royal Naval Reserve, a certain number had served during the First World War and others were joining the Navy for the first time. They were given the rank of Skipper-Lieutenant, R.N.R.

When a mine was spotted the skipper gave the order 'Out Sweep!' The mine's position was marked with a buoy, local sea traffic diverted, and if necessary the nearest port was closed. A priority message was sent to the Minesweeping Division at the Admiralty, which was responsible for all vessels. The information was checked and then broadcast to shore stations and ships at sea. Patrol vessels were posted near to the area to warn those who might not have received the message. The *Manual of Minesweeping* (1940) says that trawlers employed on war duties were 'auxiliary minesweepers'. Their objective was to:

> '...discover the presence of enemy mines or to confirm their absence; to define the limits of an area in which such mines have been laid; to provide safe channel for traffic through such an area; to remove all mines from an area.'

When a trawler on war duty destroyed a mine the crew added it to their tally. The record of mines destroyed was kept by a system of chevrons and stars painted on the trawler's side. The Minesweeping Division was responsible for all vessels and material. In the Operations Room a permanent watch plotted the movements of minesweepers and recorded the position of every mine the enemy was known to have laid, and of every ship known to have been mined. Fishermen were, of course, exceptionally sea-wise. Their experience at sea served them well for such hazardous duties and this was acknowledged by the Navy and Admiralty.

In a tough industry, life during wartime added to the immeasurable hardships. There were, as Annie Bell remembers good times to be had for Grimsby fishermen in the know especially if they had a few quid in their pockets.

> 'They was coming in and landing the fish and getting paid for it, ya know, settled. Well there was them great big water pipes you know – all the way along outside *The Telegraph*. Everybody used to fall over them at night cause it was a black out. Pubs was open while ten o'clock, and some was closed, some was open. The fish & chip shop was open so they all used to congregate there. And then there was the illegal clubs up Cleethorpes. And then there was an illegal club at Humber Street, you had to go in the back way and they'd sell you booze till 'bout two or three in the morning. You'd go down a big alley to the back of the shop - the front of the shop would be the bond. But it was made habitable, it was like a big sitting room you know and there was crates and crates of beer. It was over the odds, like, you paid but you got it. And then there was a gambling place, baccorat and dice and cards, booze and God knows what... and the

> fishermen all used to go there if they had 'owt. If you like a rag and tag town, if you know what I mean, this was it.'

Trawlers on their way to fishing grounds still faced the dangers of rough seas, appalling weather conditions, and the danger of running aground, but this was now compounded by the constant threat of enemy attack. Two thirds of English and Welsh trawlers were reputedly lost through enemy action whilst fishing.

Joan Harrison's father was one of those who continued fishing throughout the war.

> 'The only time he ever talked about his war experiences was being dive-bombed in the North Sea on their way home. He said he was terrified because he couldn't swim. When they were fishing in Iceland, they used to wait there for a convoy to bring them home. They had to wait for all the trawlers to come together. The Americans were stationed there and they were allowed to buy things from the canteen. I think I was the only girl in Grimsby with silk stockings. He used to bring home material for dresses, and flour and things. The first time I saw a white fiver was when the war started, just after and my dad came up from dock with a five pound note. They'd had a good trip and he said, "Have you ever seen one of these before?" And I hadn't, all I'd ever seen was pennies.'

At least four deep-water trawlers continued to fish from Grimsby. Armed with Lewis guns, they fished with no escort. Early opinion was divided as to whether trawlers should be armed at all. Skippers were generally against it since German aircraft could outrange Lewis guns, rendering them largely ineffective. It was argued that when a trawler had her gear down she became unable to manoeuvre and was an open target for bombers. It was feared that arming fishing vessels would invite trouble. Others, usually those who had fished in the First World War, believed they should be armed, '...better that than be shot down like rabbits.'

With fewer boats fishing, catches were good and trawlers packed double the normal capacity into their holds. The men on these vessels kept up a gruelling routine, fishing throughout the war with only 36 hours between trips as opposed to the 60 hour break during peace time.

Grimsby's first trawler loss of the war was the *Lynx II* on 28 October 1939. A minesweeper owned by Sir Thomas Robinson and Sea (Grimsby) Ltd, she was on her way to the northern fishing grounds when she picked up the distress signals of a Hull trawler, *St Nidan,* which was under attack by a German U-boat. *Lynx* pulled alongside the badly damaged *St Nidan* but she too was subjected to prolonged enemy attack. The crew members of both trawlers boarded their lifeboats and managed to escape with relatively few injuries. The crew watched as the *Lynx* refused to sink and a party from the U-boat boarded, presumably to lay charges as afterwards the *Lynx* went down.

The *Wigmore* torpedoed November 1939

Jean Teasdale (nee Ottley) and her sister Sheila were two of nine children. On 18 November 1939, their father's trawler *Wigmore* was making for Iceland when it was torpedoed, killing all on board. If making ends meet had been difficult for Jean and Sheila's mother before, it was about to become even tougher.

> 'Mother had a very hard life. She once told me it was twelve shillings and sixpence a week she got for us all to live on. She used to have to knit slippers; we never had shoes, for a long, long time, because she couldn't afford it. Thick, with thick knitting, and then she put this cardboard inside – they didn't last long! And that's how she were doing each week and keeping us, and we had to hand clothes down, y'know, like that, until we got going.'

Sheila picks up their story, remembering the day her father's ship went down.

> 'I came home from school and found lots of relatives in our living room - grandma and auntie who lived in Rotherham and those who lived in Grimsby. Usually when granny and granddad came to visit it was a happy time but no one was smiling. I asked if I could go out to play and was told I had to stay in. So I cried for no other reason than I wasn't allowed to go out - most of the people there were crying anyway. In the end I was told to go and play after all. Everything was as it always was. We were all fed, washed and ready for bed. The next day at school I was told by one of the girls that my dad was dead. I said, "No he isn't, he's at sea." We

hadn't been told anything about our dad or all the other dads. When we went home for dinner I told my mother what this girl had said and then mother said, "She's right, he is." And that was it – no explanation.

'Christmas was getting closer and we'd been told not to expect much, but people began to send money to Grimsby and a fund was opened for all the families who had lost husbands and sons and brothers. That Christmas was the best of our lives, we had toys, new clothes and shoes; we'd never had that ever before. We were even taken to a pantomime, the tickets must have been sent by someone because my mother couldn't have paid for us all to go to the theatre. It was magical, the first we'd ever seen.

'After that, things got back to normal apart from the air raids. We'd go in the shelter frightened to death night after night. We didn't like it at all but we had to go. Our eldest sister, she used to say, "If I've got to die and they drop a bomb on the bedroom – I'm staying in bed." When the all clear went, we could go back to bed. We used to find big pieces of shrapnel and jagged lumps of metal in the garden.'

In terms of losses, 1940 and 1941 were the worst years of the war for the fishing industry. The experience of the Grimsby trawler *Russell* was not unusual. She had a nine man crew and was fishing with her trawl down when she came under machine-gun fire from a German aircraft in January 1940. Afterwards in an interview with the *Grimsby Evening Telegraph*, Skipper Bert Bridges told how he and his crew and endured six attacks from a height of some 50 feet before they decided to launch the lifeboat. As they pulled away from the trawler, Bridges reported that the Germans dropped a number of light bombs and two heavy ones, all of which missed. A number of incendiary bombs were also dropped, but they flared up for 10 minutes without causing any real damage. The German plane circled the burning trawler and its crew before flying away. The crew waited, fearful that some of the bombs dropped might have had timing devices. After some 20 minutes, they re-boarded and returned the *Russell* safely home where she was repaired and carried on fishing until after the war.

Other trawlers were not so fortunate. There were six women widowed when Grimsby trawler *Leo* was given up as officially lost on 20 January 1943 with its crew of 11 men.

Annie Bell's father was the skipper-lieutenant of the trawler, *Iranian*. His orders had come directly from the Admiralty until one occasion between trips he encountered the controversial figure of Commander Lionel 'Buster' Crabb.

'Me father didn't know this bloke and he was asking a lot of questions. Where did he fish? Where did he go? And my father said, "Well we've always fished off Heligoland because there's more sole there and crayfish." So he asked was there any inlet to land in Germany or any coves a ship could go for bad weather. My father was a bit wary you know and he didn't know this man was a Commander - he thought he was just an ordinary feller and he reported him and they said they'd look into it.

'About five or six months later, not long after my father got back from Dunkirk, a civilian came to the house with two naval pickets. Me mother asked me dad what he'd been up to, and he said, "I ain't been up to nothing, I'm on leave." So this bloke's stood at the door with these two naval pickets and said they wanted me father out of the Navy to go back fishing. They said because he was an experienced skipper. He'd still have full Navy pay and what he earned from fishing. He said he'd think about it.

'He did two or three trips and this civilian bloke come back. He told me and me mother we'd have to leave so he could talk to me father in private. When we come back dad said he'd been issued with a revolver and that he was going back fishing. They'd released him to go on a ship. He said, "They're putting a gun on board, for when I leave here with the convoys. I've got to make me way to Portsmouth with the *Iranian,* and pick some bloke up and take 'im wherever he says he's got to go."

'Well when the bloke comes on board, my father said he got the fright of his life - it was that Commander Crabb. He hadn't known who he was, didn't even know he was a diver. He seemed to single me father out all the time, and it didn't matter where. He would go the pub with the lads, mucking in with his crew, and Crabb'd come over and buy them all a round of drinks and he'd say, "Come on Dick, we'll go sit on our own, I want to know more about this fishing." My father said there was something not right. Anyway he took him wherever he had to go and when he came back he said to me mam, "I'm bloody sure there's something wrong. I don't know what it is, I'm not sure of that bloke at all." Anyway, they went out, made the trip and come in, and went out again, and he said, "I've

The *Iranian* lost 12 January 1944

got an awful feeling." Me mother asked what he meant and he said, "I don't know, it's a messy feeling. I don't like him asking all these questions."

'My old man he was on a minesweeper - two or three used to go out everyday to clear from the dock gates right through the channel, right through the Humber. Anyway, my father goes on this trip with Crabb and when my old man come in dock, he come and found me in the Kent Arms where I was working as a barmaid. He said, "Your father isn't coming home Anne." I said, "What d'you mean?" He said, "We've been and fetched the ships in but three of em's gone over, torpedoed. We escorted them to the mouth of the Humber, and then we had to go out on patrol again. But we knew there were no mines, 'cause we'd cleared the Humber, there were no mines at all."

'About three months after that, me mother applied for a widows' pension. At first they said it was out of their hands, they could do nothing about it. Then this bloke came from the Admiralty, he said, "Don't worry about money because he's still on a big Navy pension. You'll get that the rest of your life, and if there's anything you want, you've only got to write to this address." I don't know what it was, and he said, "He'll be commended for what he's done." Me mother asked, what did he do? He said it was confidential and we'd not get to know.

'When I got married a few year after, my old man got in touch with someone in London, in the Admiralty and asked them for information of how the ships went. And they said they couldn't give no information because they were just classed as missing, but me husband told them in the letter that he was on the ship and he's seen the ships go up when the torpedoes hit. I think it's only fair that the families of the rest of them should know, I want them to know that them ships never went into a minefield, they were torpedoed.'

As the war continued so did the decline in the numbers of men fishing: only 25% of the English and Welsh trawler fleet was available. The Admiralty had requisitioned the larger vessels, catching power was much less and a large area of the North Sea was closed to shipping. By then, British fishermen had also been joined by allies from further afield as Allison Josefsen remembers.

> 'My grandfather was Danish and he came over from the war. He was a fisherman in Denmark and he came over to Whitehaven. He had a machine gun on top of his wheel house. And he fought the Germans. He helped the British. There's not many of the old Danish fishermen left now, but that's how they came over to Whitehaven first and then they moved here to Grimsby.'

By 1944, fishing was at 48% of the pre-war total. Interviewed in the *Grimsby Evening Telegraph*, Mr J. Vincent, chairman of the Grimsby United Fish Merchants and Fish Curers Association, said:

> 'Grimsby fish merchants are alarmed at the serious effect on their customers' trade by the recent embargo and consequent high prices.'

As the roles of Grimsby fishermen changed during the war, so too did the role of women employed in the industry. Net braiders played a crucial part in the war effort and were aided by the Grimsby Corporation in getting orders for camouflage netting, with strips of drab-coloured material running through the meshes of the nets. Grimsby still had 250 net braiders working primarily for the fishing fleet during the war.

In 1940, the Grimsby Fishermen's Auxiliary War Fund had been established to relieve the hardship of widows and families of fishermen lost in minesweeping and other services during the war. When war was declared, the Government decided that dependents of fishermen lost through enemy action should be entitled to the same pension as men on active service. In light of this, Dependents' Fund trustees resolved that should there be any delay in the payment of government pensions, relief would be paid anyway.

The war was desperately costly in terms of men and ships lost. The *Grimsby Evening Telegraph* reported 119 fishing boats from Grimsby as war losses. In the first year of the conflict 59 minesweeping trawlers and drifters were lost at sea, 34 of which were struck by mines. Overall, between 1939 and 1945, Grimsby lost 600 fishermen. Their role did not go unnoticed or unrewarded, and by the end of

1946, 73 fishermen who had not been on naval service were awarded MBEs, whilst another 90 received the British Empire Medal (BEM) for actions in war. Those employed in minesweeping duties were recognised by Winston Churchill:

> 'A significant proportion of our whole war effort had to be devoted to combating the mine. A vast output of material and money was diverted from other tasks, and many thousands of men risked their lives night and day in the minesweepers alone.'

Indeed, the role fishermen played during the war, whether as a continuation of their fishing duties or as auxiliaries to the Royal Navy, was crucial to Britain's war effort. Their service and sacrifice is commemorated in the Royal Naval Patrol Service Veteran's War Memorial paid for by veterans close to the Queen's Steps on Grimsby's Royal Dock.

Deslys Fairfield's father went to sea in 1931. He was called up and didn't return home until the war ended.

> 'I didn't see much of me dad during the war 'cos he was away, South Africa and places like that. I can remember him coming home and I hadn't seen him really since the war started and I shouted, "Mam there's a man coming up the yard." And she said, "It's your daddy."'

Sadly, the losses continued right up until the end of the war as Mike Connor remembers, his family were celebrating VE Day on 8 May 1945.

> 'I just remember we was all enjoying ourselves at me mother's house and a chap came to the door with a black suit, black cap. He was the Port Missioner, he'd come to tell me mother and me grandmother that they'd found the wreckage of me Grandfather Connor's ship – they'd hit a mine and it was all blown to pieces. And I remember them all crying and… everybody was celebrating the end of the war. But three Grimsby trawlers were lost at the same time. Seventy-five men were lost. Seventy-five bread winners. It was the steam trawler *Devonshire* and it was lost. Me grandmother was never the same again, she ended up in a home. It knocked the stuffing out of her. You see the men lost their lives but the women had it for the rest of their lives.'

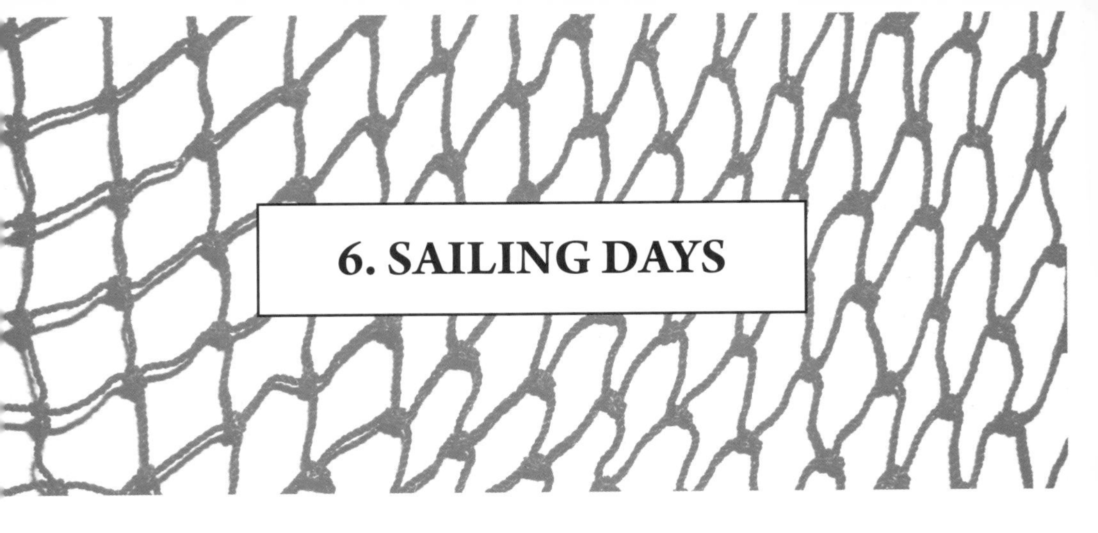

6. SAILING DAYS

'I never watched him go away...'

Each family had their rituals for sailing day, the things they'd pack in the kitbag, the same cab driver waiting at the gate. It was considered bad luck to watch the men leave. Rita Whittle wouldn't watch as her husband went away.

> 'You never stood at the window and saw them go. You never washed on the day they went to sea, never wash them away. You never wore anything green and they'd never take anything green with them. We never parted if we'd had a few words, you'd settle it, say sorry. I've known ships miss a tide over that. It was a life of trust; they had to trust us being away all that time. I used to write letters, care of the pilot station, when they went to the White Sea. We could send wires, like a telegram, for birthdays. I had a code book and it was so much a word and I used to code the messages. We had a code between us. They used to sell the books at Burnetts in Riby Square. It was like

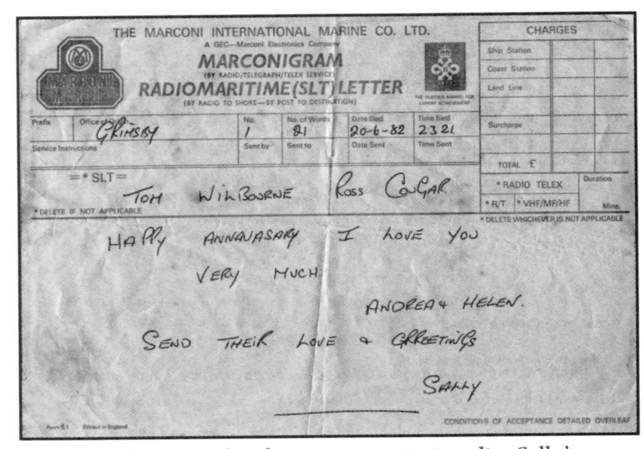

THE MARCONI INTERNATIONAL MARINE CO. LTD.
A GEC—Marconi Electronics Company
MARCONIGRAM
(BY RADIO/TELEGRAPH/TELEX SERVICE)
RADIOMARITIME (SLT) LETTER
(BY RADIO TO SHORE—BY POST TO DESTINATION)

Prefix	Office of Origin	No.	No. of Words	Date filed	Time filed
	GRIMSBY	1	21	20-6-82	2321
Service Instructions		Sent by	Sent to	Date Sent	Time Sent

CHARGES	
Ship Station	
Coast Station	
Land Line	
Surcharge	
TOTAL £	

=* SLT=
TOM WILBOURNE ROSS COUGAR
* DELETE IF NOT APPLICABLE

* RADIO TELEX | * R/T | * VHF/MF/HF | Duration Mins.
* DELETE WHICHEVER IS NOT APPLICABLE

HAPPY ANNIVERSARY I LOVE YOU
VERY MUCH.
ANDREA & HELEN.
SEND THEIR LOVE & GREETINGS
SALLY

CONDITIONS OF ACCEPTANCE DETAILED OVERLEAF

An example of a message sent via radio: Sally's anniversary message to her husband Tom

> a private way of talking to each other, but it depended on the wireless operator on the ship.'

As Angela McMullen remembers, watching her father leave home could be a painful experience, but one which you were expected to accept without complaint.

> 'I know I played up once and said I didn't want him to go and I started to cry and me mother told me off. I only did it the once. She said it wasn't fair.'

In the days before technology made instant contact and a ready supply of information possible, Angela remembers how the haunting tones of the shipping forecast was the only link to her father at sea.

> 'We always listened to the shipping forecast - in fact I can still remember it. And when we heard the bad weather we always said our prayers every night. It was part of it. There's a faith within the fishing fraternity, it's not the one like going to church but I don't think there's anyone that sailed out of this port that hasn't got some form of faith that they feel there is someone out there hopefully looking out for them. So we prayed. And me father would say, don't listen to the forecast. He said the winds on shore are a different type to the winds of the sea. And he said when we're in a gale it's better to go into the teeth of it than have it behind you, cause that way it's more dangerous. But we still listened to the radio.'

Like most fishermen, Angela's father said little about his time away.

> 'You get two types of trawlermen. One that would open up and say what happens and the others that just get on with it. We used to get to know far more from the chap next door. He told me mother there'd been a hatchet fight on board ship! She hadn't known about it. The only time he said something was when he was off watch and there was a fire in the engine room and the young lad who was the fireman he went to get in the lifeboat. So me father you know had to put it out and douse it all down, and it was pretty dangerous. But instead of helping, this lad was doing a runner for the lifeboat. So I mean we got to know that obviously as it was a fire. But he never said anything about the fights on board, you know. I suppose being in close proximity with everyone you're bound to get on each others nerves sometimes.
>
> 'We had a big brown suitcase. We'd keep the *Evening Telegraph* and

anything that my mother thought would be interesting she'd put a cross at the top and highlight it so when me father came home from sea he had this great big pile of newspapers to go through. And he would read through and catch up on what'd been happening in the town while he was away. Later on he bought a Grundig tape recorder and so he could have some music to listen to. Of course it was pretty primitive. But me father was an engineer six hours on, six hours off for the whole trip so he wouldn't have had much spare time.'

For fishing families, the cycle of sailing, the weeks without husband or father, and then the brief return, began the day the ship sailed. But as Mike Connor remembers, not every fisherman was ready and willing to return to sea. His uncle Jack was at times a reluctant fisherman.

'He always used to sneak round to our house. You always knew when he was due for sailing 'cause he was there. There was a knock at the door three o'clock one morning and he said, "Tell the runner I'm not here." The runner said, "Is your Uncle Jack here young Connor?" I said he wasn't and the runner said, "Yes he is." He barged past me, shouting, "C'mon Jack you've gotta sail. If you don't go I'll have you walking about for three months." That meant he'd stop you getting a ship for three months.

'The runner was one of the most important jobs in Grimsby. I wouldn't want that job - can you imagine trying to get a bloke out at three in the morning who's in bed with his wife, he's half drunk anyway, and tell him he's gotta go on a freezing ship to Iceland. Who the hell would wanna get out of bed? They didn't actually knock 'em over the head like they did in the eighteenth century, but it's not far off. They used to threaten them, what he did was ring up all the firms and say Jack Swan, he wouldn't come to sea and they put the kibosh on him for three months. He couldn't get a ship and he was nearly poverty stricken.'

Pete Woods sailed as a young deckhand and remembers the police being brought to the dockside to search the crew for drink.

'I hardly ever sailed sober off shore, ever. And I don't remember going on a ship where any of the deckies were sober. The runner would come for you and say there was ten ships going, twenty men on each, that's two-hundred people. Well out of them there was only ten deckies on each and it was the deckies that were normally the trouble on the North Wall.

You used to stand on the wall seeing your mates before you went. And you always had a can of beer in your hand and a bottle of rum in your pocket or whatever. Then you'd stagger aboard and off you go. But once we sailed and we got out the river, the old man set the watches and the first thing we used to do, we used to call it the party berth, whichever was the biggest berth on the ship all the deckies used to pile in there and we all used to take booze away with us and get rip-roaring drunk, fight, knock the shit out of each other.'

For Olga Drever, an afternoon pleasure trip on her husband's ship turned into more of a voyage that she'd planned.

'I went out in the Humber with Steve's brother who was a skipper. The lads on the ship hauled me and the mate's wife - my husband was bosun then - on the ship at the lock gates. Colin, my husband's brother, said he'd take us out as far as Spurn and then bring us back. But it didn't work out like that because there was a lot of work to be done on the ship y'see. So Colin thought it'd be alright and he'd drop us off at Scarborough. Well I'm on the deck in high-heeled shoes filling needles, because I used to be a needle-filler at Cosalt and Tanning in Ropery Street. Anyway, we got dropped off in Scarborough because Colin had had enough of us and he knew a chappie who'd got a boat and he come out and picked us up. I'd left my two children with my mother-in-law, and my sister-in-law who was Colin's wife had left four children so there were six kids with my mother-in-law. I tell you we got into so much trouble. The taxi driver who dropped us off at the docks, we had him regular, we left all our handbags in his car because we only thought we'd be going aboard at the lock gates and Louie, they called him Louie, he took all our handbags back home to my mother-in-law. And she said, "Well, where are they?" Louie said, "Oh they've gone out to sea with Colin." Well she went beserk, saying she was going to get the authorities and everything. But the kids were well looked after and we were only away overnight. One of the lads on the ship said, that was the first time he'd seen a deckie with high-heeled shoes on.'

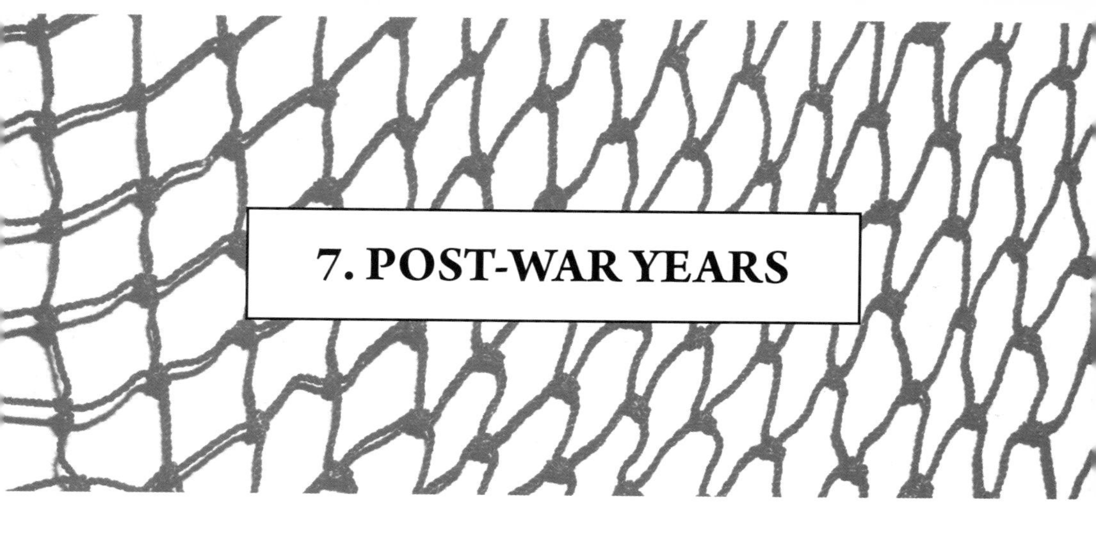

7. POST-WAR YEARS

'Harry was on board the trawler that was captured by the Russians...'

The years immediately following the Second World War were some of the industry's worst since the 1920s. The Second World War had created years of enforced conservation. Fish stocks recovered and fishermen returned in increasing numbers to old fishing grounds. Food shortages and rationing increased demand for unrationed fish sold at prices set by the Ministry of Food, but the relative boom disguised the industry's problems. The North Sea was showing signs of decline as early as the end of 1946 and fish prices collapsed in November 1949, a few months after the Government removed price controls.

Increases in distant water landings, imports, food shortages and rationing, brought unemployment to near and middle-waters. In response, the Government created the White Fish Authority which, alongside the Herring Industry Board, was responsible for overseeing grants, loans, and subsidies aimed at restoring the productivity of near and middle-water fleets.

There were a number of significant and well-publicised losses. In September 1953, five Grimsby fishermen were lost on board the trawler *Hassett* when it hit rocks at Auckingill, north of Wick, Caithness. In response to radio calls, the destroyer H.M.S *Scorpion* rushed to the scene. The rescue operation was delayed however as it took four hours for the Wick lifeboat to locate the troubled trawler. The coastguard was asked to assist the lifeboat when heavy seas prevented it from getting near

Hassett on the rocks near Auckinghill. 18 September 1953

the trawler, which was by this time awash. The lifeboat fired two lines across the vessel but the crew members who had managed to get to the bridge could not reach them. Subsequently, two of the lifeboat crew went onto the rocks and fired three lines, one of which the mate managed to secure. The bodies of three crew members were picked up as the lifeboat returned to her station. A combined funeral service was conducted by Albert Broughton, Port Missioner for Grimsby. The *Hassett* was a total loss with heavy gales and bad seas preventing any salvage operation.

On 18 January 1954, the *Laforey* sailed from Grimsby for the Norwegian coast grounds, and was homeward bound with a catch of 1,500 kits when she ran aground four miles south-west of Kvalholmen Lighthouse, near the port of Floroe. The trawler released the following message: '*Laforey Laforey Laforey*, we are ashore at Yttero. We are ashore at Yttero. We need immediate assistance.' Not long afterwards, a second distress call was received. Nothing else was heard from the trawler and at midnight on 8 February she capsized, resulting in the death of all 20 crew members. The rescue vessels were led by Grimsby trawler *Stockham,* which had picked up the SOS.

The Alicon Stove

Weather

Lighting-up

Grimsby Evening Telegraph

Final

Edwards for Paint

Twopence

GRIMSBY TRAWLER UPSIDE DOWN

Silence after Laforey SOS : 'Listing heavily—capsizing'

SHIP SIGHTS WRECK–BUT NO SIGN YET OF CREW OF 20

THE Grimsby trawler Laforey, which last night sent an SOS saying she was capsizing, was sighted today lying bottom up on a reef off the Norwegian coast. There was no sign of any of the crew of 20.

Skipper W. Mogg

Stockham races to aid

Mr. K. Mogg

THE MEN OF THE LAFOREY

Mate with skipper father

The Grimsby trawler Laforey.

Girl of 11 found strangled in flat

Dawson tries to buy steak

HUMBER

RAIL BRIDGE CRASHES ON LINCS. LINE

PROMPT action saved a train-load of passengers and three pedestrians when almost 90ft. of the 300ft. long concrete footbridge over the Cleethorpes-Doncaster railway line collapsed at Scunthorpe yesterday.

STRATOJET CRASHES: THREE DIE

A memorial service for all 20 men was held on 17 February, and was attended by almost 1,000 people, 300 of whom were relatives of the lost men. Every section of the fishing industry and public life of the town was represented. Many members of the public were unable to gain admission and along with several hundred others could only watch the arrival of mourners in Duncombe Street.

In 1956, Grimsby's fishing industry celebrated its centenary. The local press published supplements full of stories about the industry's growth and development. It could not have come at a better time as the 1950s witnessed a revival in the fishing industry which lasted until 1961 when Britain yielded to Iceland's demands following the first cod war.

An important year in the industry's development, 1957 saw a number of trawler firms merging to form bigger groups. One of the most significant was the purchase of Butt Groups Ltd. by Northern Trawlers Ltd. This gave Northern Trawlers the biggest fleet in the port. Similarly, one of Grimsby's oldest trawler owners, T. C & F. Moss Ltd. disappeared as a company when it was purchased by the Ross Group Ltd.

Losses at sea were fewer that year, and it was the second successive year that no fishermen had been killed as a result of a shipwreck; although four men were lost through the day to day hazards of fishing. The year witnessed a change in trawling regulations, and it was made legal for trawlers to carry rubber dinghies as opposed to the traditional lifeboat. In 1958, the Queen visited Grimsby and was taken on a tour of the dock.

The Queen, Duke of Edinburgh and Lord Ancastor at Grimsby Royal Dock Basin

Joan Harrison's father had been second engineer on trawlers most of his working life. He retired in 1945. His sons began fishing after the war when ships faced new the hazards of the Cold War.

> 'My brother Harry was on board the trawler that was captured by the Russians. It was fishing too near the coast; I think it was the Buffalo. They had the whole crew in prison for a few weeks.'

Cold War relations had tragic consequences for Emma Brennan's brother, John who had not long started fishing when he was involved in an accident.

> 'John went to sea and I think he did three trips, this was in 1947. The *Pataudi* they called the trawler and he was fishing on the deck and something happened – a wire took his leg off. It was when there was a cold war and they went to Russia to see if they could get him into a hospital but the Russians didn't want to know. So he had to steam all the way back to Norway to get him into a hospital there. By that time John had lost too much blood. He died. He was about twenty-seven.'

Such tragedies continued in peacetime as they had in times of war. Fishing went on and communities grieved and coped with social and political change. But while business was booming, an ongoing dispute between Britain and Iceland regarding fishery limits was beginning to gather momentum. Trouble between British and Icelandic fishermen had existed ever since the development of the northern fishing grounds. Most of the trouble had been between individual boats with the odd trawler being arrested for illegal fishing inside national territorial waters (the original three mile limit). In these incidents the skipper would be fined and his catch confiscated. It had never been an international issue, but this changed in 1958 when Iceland unilaterally extended her fishery limits from three to 12 miles.

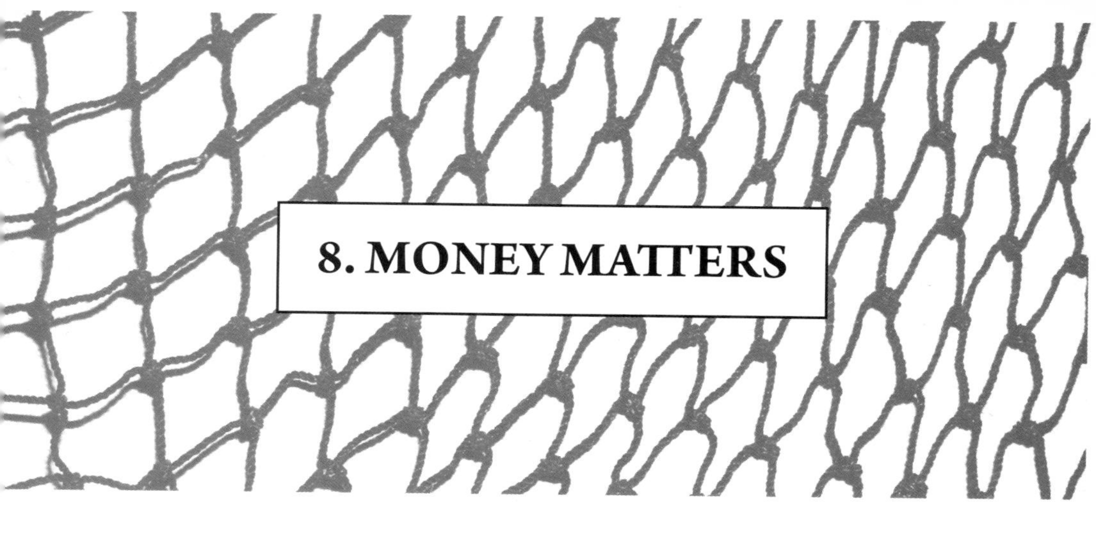

8. MONEY MATTERS

'Do we owe your mam anything this trip?'

The struggle to cope alone for many women came down to a single issue: money. For fishing families, financial security fluctuated as it always had done, trip by trip, catch by catch. Sally Wilbourne's husband was never on a top-earning ship, which meant that getting by wasn't easy.

> 'The only time quite honestly that we really started to feel safe financially was when the industry collapsed and he went to work for Cosalt. And we had a regular wage and he couldn't believe it, you know every week he used to get his wage packet and it was so much more than he'd ever earned at sea. It was the best time because we had a regular wage coming in and he was at home every night, but we were too old to appreciate it.
>
> 'Our wages were paid back out of any settlings, whatever it was, no matter how small. The four pounds, ten shillings a week I got was taken out of whatever profit there was when the fish was sold. If he made a bad trip, the owners would still take back the wages. Tom's first thing when we'd settled up after a good trip was to go to the bank and put some into a current account for our overheads you know, household bills and that. And then it was, *what did the children need for school?* Whatever they wanted for school we made sure they had it. Sometimes we used to end up with very little and you couldn't go out and you couldn't have any sort of pleasure, because the money was basically spoken for.

In the days before the war, Margaret Monger's father John Calver Monger went to sea. Starting out as an apprentice, he made sure his family was well looked-after. Margaret still lives in the house her father bought.

> 'In the days I'm talking about, fishermen's wives had two pounds a week from their husband's firm. We used to finish school at two o'clock on a Friday so the fishermen's wives could go down the docks and pick up their money, though my mother had hers delivered – I assume my dad paid for the runner to bring the wages up – she wasn't the only one, quite a few of them did. Then when the men came back and settled, out of what the settlings were, they had to pay back that two pounds and then they got whatever was left. So you've been at sea for twenty-eight or thirty days for maybe a few pounds. Having said that, my dad bought this house for five-hundred pounds, which was a lot in 1931. He worked out that by the time he'd paid for the house he'd have paid twice as much, so for the next two years, he saved his money and bought the house outright in 1933. We did have to pay ground rent to Sidney Sussex College until he retired at sixty-two and then he bought the freehold. As far as my mother was concerned, she did all the bills, they were all in her name anyway.'

Ann Graves remembers the Friday afternoon trip to the Duncombe Street offices to pick up the family's weekly money. Some 40 years after Margaret's father managed to buy his house, the fishermen's wage was still barely enough to live on.

> 'I had to sign for a little brown envelope. I think we started off on about eleven or twelve pounds a week and it was about thirteen when he died. When he was in, the pay was mine for the housekeeping and the bills – you did everything. Nothing came out of the housekeeping. If we needed a loaf of bread, if we needed vegetables, he paid for the lot. After a couple of years he used to come in and say, "Do we owe your mam anything this trip?" And I'd say we owed her five bob for whatever, half a dollar, two and sixpence. If I ever owed any money to my mother or if he thought I did, he gave it to her and then he'd buy me anything I wanted, but he wouldn't give me any money. So the money that he thought he owed me mother, *that* was mine. Crafty, but that's the way it was.'

The Friday afternoon trip to pick up the wages took on legendary status as Mike Connor remembers.

'It was called the Fish Dock Races. And they all used to go, although my mother never did, she had that many kids, so Auntie Anna used to go and fetch the wages. They all used to give her half a crown and she used to collect the wages for about seven or eight different ladies. She made a pound – doesn't sound a lot now but it was in them days. It was very tight. I was brought up on ration books. And that was my job every Saturday to take the ration books in. My mother used to trade, see we had a lot of fish in our house. Every Saturday me grandmother used to give me these parcels of fish and say, "Take this one to Mrs Snyder, that one to Mrs West, and don't you dare tell anybody." Off Mrs West I'd perhaps get a load of sugar, off Mrs Snyder a load of butter. But it was illegal, black market. There were no men there and the women had to do that to get by. The ration didn't supply enough margarine or sugar. So they had to swap, barter and exchange and that's how they got by. There was even a shop that used to sell horse meat; I actually used to eat horse meat as a kid and tripe. And we also used to eat rabbit every Sunday, that was our staple diet on a Sunday dinner. You could only afford chicken at Christmas.

'There was a shop called The Lion Clothing Company near the docks and every trip me dad used to give them so much and then me mother could go and get us our clothes. She was permanently in hock for years, but it was the only way she could clothe us. And then if we needed a pair of shoes we used to go to The Lion Clothing Company. There was no such thing as going with cash, there's no chance of that. You just couldn't do it then. Not just my mother, everyone was like that.'

Deslys Fairfield's mother managed to make sure the money her father gave her stretched to meet their needs. Like many families, they used 'tickets' to buy what they needed.

'I suppose the odd thing like that we'd do at Lawson and Stockdales. It wasn't easy I shouldn't think, but me mother was a good manager and a marvellous cook. My dad would go and have a drink and then come back. He liked to have a little flutter on the 'orses but he wouldn't use money that me mother needed. He never spent money that was needed in the home. As soon as my dad got his wages she got hers. Let's face it, in those days people was rich or just ordinary. But we never went without anything really. I mean I'm not saying we had sixty-four frocks each or owt like that. But I mean me mother was a very astute woman and as I say me dad he never left her short of money. If he came in and picked up his wages he'd take his spending money out and me mother got the rest.'

Marjorie Louis would buy the cheapest cuts of meat to make sure there was food on the table

'You got a pig's fry for half a crown, and you got liver, sausage, pork chop, belly pork, kidney. And you did two meals with that for two days. My son always said, "We had stew, but there was no meat in it." We'd queue on the market to get a rabbit for about two shillings. All dressed and skinned and everything. You were only allowed two and the queue used to be right round the market. Rabbit was a luxury.'

Marjorie's daughter Lorraine and her brothers would have their main meal at school. Tea at home was something on toast, sandwiches or corned beef hash. Treats were few and far between.

'We used to go on the boating lake and the open air bathing pool with a bottle of water and some bread and butter and that was our dinner. I remember coming home from an afternoon swimming, all starving, and we used to go round the back of the Kingsway Hotel, knock on the door and the chef used to come and he'd give us their crusts - all their crusts used to have butter on, which we didn't have. We used to go down the street eating these crusts. When the ice cream man came, mum used to say, "Go and ask him if him if he's got any broken cornets." Or she'd give us two shillings and send us to the Waverley for stale cakes. Aunt Cis lived down the road, and whenever she come to our house me mam would make her a cup of tea, but we could never afford chocolate biscuits and Aunt Cis always loved chocolate biscuits with her cup of tea, so she fetched her own in a little parcel and we'd sit and watch her.'

Like many fishermen's wives, Doreen Tyson's mother brought up her family in what was essentially a lone-parent household. It was a lifestyle the family were used to, but meant making sure there was money to pay the bills. This was difficult enough, but when at the age of 11, Doreen passed a scholarship to the local technical school, finding the money for a school uniform made extra demands on the family finances.

'Somehow or other she got the money together and bought my school uniform. In those days it was quite common for families to shop with a ticket and it was quite a regular thing in our house. Things were rationed and were hard to come by. It's a strange sort of period we're talking about; in the late 40s and 50s everybody was more or less in the same situation. You never had anything more than your neighbour had.

'Generosity is another thing about fishermen. Most fishermen would give their last penny away. My mother would be home and my dad had probably gone down to settle up. He started as a deck hand and finished up as a skipper, but he was never ever a top earner and they'd say, "Bet Sam's in the pub. He's settled up and he's had a good trip." And she used to scoot down to try and find him before he spent it all. She needed things for the home and he never gave that a thought, because he'd never had to deal with the accounting – my mother did it all. Women generally are better at organising the housekeeping money and my mother certainly needed it, she had a growing family.'

There were few ways for a trawlerman to increase his money other than to take his mate's or skipper's ticket. It was the same for those below decks, any progression involved taking six weeks ashore to study and take exams. For some families, the six weeks without earning was an insurmountable barrier. The family finances simply could not cope with the loss of earnings. Josephine Gibney's husband began below decks as a fireman.

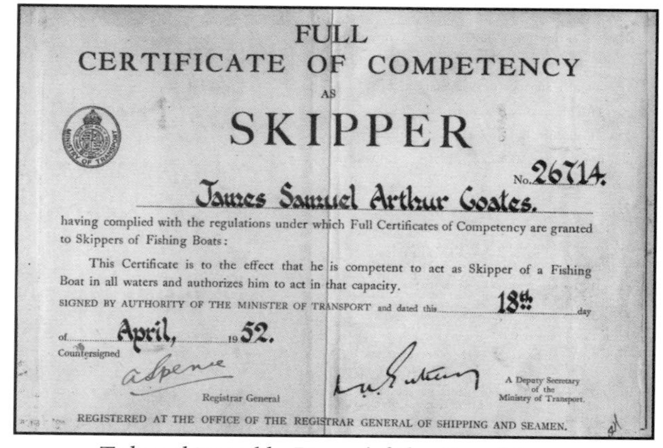
FULL
CERTIFICATE OF COMPETENCY
AS
SKIPPER

No. 26714.

James Samuel Arthur Coates.

having complied with the regulations under which Full Certificates of Competency are granted to Skippers of Fishing Boats:

This Certificate is to the effect that he is competent to act as Skipper of a Fishing Boat in all waters and authorizes him to act in that capacity.

SIGNED BY AUTHORITY OF THE MINISTER OF TRANSPORT and dated this 18th day of April, 1952.

Countersigned

Registrar General

A Deputy Secretary of the Ministry of Transport.

REGISTERED AT THE OFFICE OF THE REGISTRAR GENERAL OF SHIPPING AND SEAMEN.

To be a skipper like Doreen's father Sam, fishermen needed to study for their ticket

'I used to say to him, "Well you're doing the chief engineer's job, why don't you sit for your ticket?" We was ever so poor like, sometimes he'd bring in about thirty shillings or two pounds up in t'North Sea. But we saved up and he took six weeks off to pass the first one, then second engineer, then third. In them days they never used to give you money to sit the tickets. We lived with me mother then and we had no money or anything.'

As Rita Whittle discovered when her husband was injured at sea, the ship owners would put a stop on fishermen's wages if they were unfit to work. Rita made the money last until her husband was able to make it home and sign on with the doctor, but as Pete Woods remembers, women had always found ways to 'get by'.

> 'Everybody knows the story about what women did with the fishermen's clothes – the suits. They'd pawn them as soon as you sailed, straight in the pawn shop and they'd get 'em out the day before you come in.'

Annie Bell had a good friend in the pawn shop before the war.

> 'Of course they weren't earning much the ships them days, and the wages wasn't much. His suit was in the pawn shop before he got out the lock pits, and his boots. We had good neighbours, you'd say, "My old man's coming in on this tide and his suit's in." Off would come the wedding ring, "Go get ten bob on the wedding and get his suit out, take it to Renos." It was one and six to have it pressed. It was all smart. As soon as he'd gone out the lock pit we'd pawn something to get her ring out for her old man coming in.
>
> 'If we got owt from the pawn shop then the rent got paid, or if we missed the rent there was two bags of coal and a bag of logs, or if the kids wanted shoes, the shoes got bought and the landlord didn't get nowt. Then we used to tick the milk until the end of the week, and then we had a book where you could go and get your rations, pay at the end of the week. It was a struggle, but we got out of it you know. Some got paid, some didn't, but it evened itself out. They didn't go short, they waited - well they had to.'

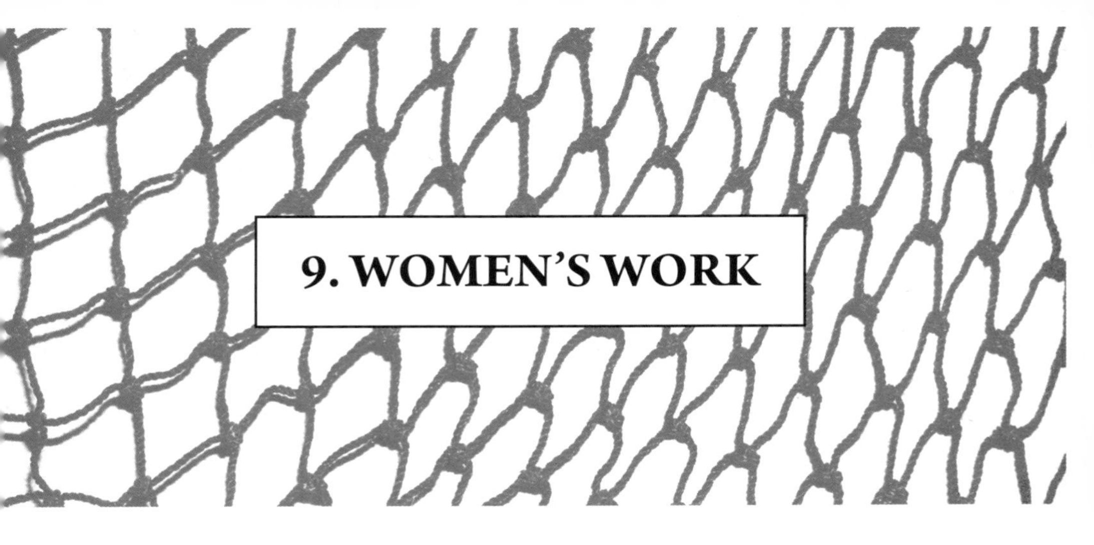

9. WOMEN'S WORK

'... a paid man's anybody's man.'

The domestic working lives of women in the fishing industry were, in many respects, the same as millions of other women across the country. However, the demands of a two or three day turnaround between trips brought its own pressures. In the days before washing machines and dryers, taking on the task of making sure her husband's sea-gear was ready for the next trip was Rita Whittle's first priority.

> 'Say my husband came in on a Sunday morning, we'd meet him at the dock, come home and have Sunday lunch and I'd start washing. No washing machines; when I was first married we had two rooms. I used a sink, a rubbing board and a table top wringer. And that was for hob wool. I used to knit his hob wool socks. I don't know if you've ever seen or smelt the sodding things, but hob wool stinks, it's oily and thick. He used to take three pairs of socks, two Guernseys – which I knitted. He had long-johns, vests with sleeves – three of each, and then a smock thing they wore. It was a heavy brown cloth all covered in blood and scales. The only thing he never brought home was his boots and waterproofs. I'd wash Sunday afternoon and evening, dry it Monday and Tuesday for him to go away in again on Wednesday morning. We used to put it across the fire guard when we had open fires. When we moved into our little house in Duncombe Street, he bought me an English Electric washer with an electric roller - an ordinary washer with an agitator. It heated the water

and it had a boiler I could use to heat water for the bath. Then years later I had twin tub – until I broke it. Then I bought a second-hand automatic for fifteen pounds. When the launderette opened I used to wash at home and put the washing in a shopping trolley and take it down there to dry.'

As a boy, Mike Connor remembers how his Aunt Anne would help his mother out on washing days.

> 'I used to hate Mondays. I'd go to school at half-past eight and me mother was getting it ready - you had to fill a copper and boil the water - and when I came home from school at half-past four they were still doing it. It was a two person job. She couldn't have done it all on her own. It was ten hours of graft. That was all me dad's fishing gear, all me brother and sister's gear. They had to wash it by hand, push it through a wringer and if it was raining, well it went into Tuesday 'cos you couldn't dry it. So sometimes it could take as long as three days just to do that. She had to have his sea gear cleaned and ready for when he went off you see. He come in with a great big black bag, stinking of fish. Apart from having a day out with him, she had to do all that and it had to be clean. It was pressure, pressure all the time on her you see but she just accepted it my mother, took it in her stride.'

There were rules about when you could and couldn't wash. On one occasion when her husband had been away, Josephine Gibney had ignored them.

> 'He came in one day and said, "Have you done the washing?" I knew what it was. There's that old superstition, you didn't wash the day they went to sea in case you washed them away, and I had. I said I hadn't. The skipper had gone mad, they'd had a rotten trip and he was ever so quiet spoken and he said, "Josie, somebody washed." I thought well they don't know it was me so I'm not saying.'

Emma Brennan's mother had fought hard to ensure her daughters were looked after. As soon as they began work they were expected to contribute to the family bills. Emma brought the same expectations to her marriage.

> 'You either worked or didn't pay your lodge and me mother wanted her money every week. When I was married, I ran the house. I'd say, "There's a bill here." He'd want to pay it tomorrow. That was his attitude, *it'll do tomorrow*. Once I asked him if I could have a new washer. He said, "Well

that's going into debt." He didn't like debt so I said I'd see about just trying to save, but by the time you'd got your pocket money saved up – I mean it was hopeless.

'I was a lollipop lady for about twenty years and I used to earn two pounds fifty a week. A lot of them were starting on at Birdseye – and I tried there for a week. But no, too much machinery and shouting and noise and I didn't want that so I went to be a lollipop lady, helping the kids across the road. And I loved it.'

In the years before the war, Annie Bell trained as a barmaid at the Oberon on Cleethorpe Road. She didn't stay long before moving on.

'I went to the Kent Arms. Then after I was married I went to the Lincoln Arms and worked there. I left there because I was bit fed up with barmaiding. You never had time for yourself. The lasses on the game, they all used to stand outside the Lincoln, waiting for one of us barmaids. "Ave yer got 'alf a crown to gerrus in? Once we're in we're alright." And I'd give 'em half a crown. The nurse used to come in for them lasses if they didn't attend the clinic. They got yanked out. There used to be a bloke, I don't know if he was a policeman or what, he'd say, "Come on, let's have yer." Out they used to go. They always knew where the lasses would be, it was either the Red Lion or the Lincoln, and there was another honky-tonk somewhere. They was worse than the lads for fighting, over blokes you know, "You slept with him last night!" Then, "So what, a paid man's anybody's man."

'Me mother was working in the fish house among the kippers, so I went down to see her one day. Brenda Fisher was the head woman there - 'er that swum the channel - and I see 'er, so she said what you doing? And I said, "I've just left me job as a barmaid, I've come to see me mam." She said, "Do you want a job?" So I said, "Yeah." She said, "Right, start in the morning."

'The 'errings was running down - I mean we used to get the herring boats come, but it declined you know so they sold out to Ross Group. Well Ross Group didn't do it like we used to. We had big tubs of brine and in the winter we had to break the ice off it. When we went to Ross Group it was all electric, steamed electric and it wasn't done like that you see. When we used to do 'em, we used to put 'em on the nails on a rod, and

Scottish herring girls, Grimsby

then there was a kiln and we used to walk each side of the kiln you know while they was still smoking, and close the doors and then get on with the job. But at Ross Group it was electric and it wasn't the same as the brining we were used to. So I left. Well we all did, those that had worked for Greens.'

Traditional women's' work allied to the fishing industry changed throughout the 20th century. The Ross food group was founded in Grimsby in 1920; Birds Eye opened their first factory in Grimsby in 1929; W Young and Son began developing frozen fish products in 1946. It was the era of processed food and through the fishing industry, and its community of women prepared to work filleting fish or on production lines, Grimsby laid claim to being at the forefront of a food revolution. Before she married, Sally Wilbourne had taken a job on the docks.

> 'I don't know how I got onto it, but I went to work fishcake packing. And it's funny because this girl's a friend now, but I went through hell - I wouldn't swear and curse like they would you see. And there was this one girl in particular, she was like a little doll you know always beautifully made up and everything whereas this friend of mine Maisie and I, we just used to get into our gear and go down and that was it. This girl though, she was always finding fault with me for some reason you know and making snide remarks about, "Some folks think they're better..." just because I didn't live in Grimsby. Luckily I had this friend and we were two of the fastest packers so we were at the top of the conveyor belt, otherwise if we'd been at the other end she'd probably have sent them all down to me. I worked down there until I was married, and I stayed part time until the children came along really. Tom's fairly strict; he wasn't here so I had to be for the kids, which was right.'

When the industry was at its peak, there was a need for companies like Cosalt and Tanning, formerly the Great Grimsby Coal, Salt and Tanning Company, to meet the equipment demands of the fishing fleet. Traditionally, many women turned to net-braiding as a source of income. Sisters Beverley Reed and Maureen Harvey were braiders. Maureen began in the 1950s. It was customary for girls to start out as needle fillers, working for more experienced braiders.

> 'When I first started needle filling we used to stand and I think we had six or eight braiders to fill for, ten minutes each and they wanted however many needles you could fill in that time. The more you could fill, the happier they were. I always remember starting and continually looking at the clock. It seemed like hours and hours and hours. And then after eighteen months you get set on as a braider. But the braiders at that time had to teach you how to do it. You had to watch them and fill your needles at the same time, and what you didn't know you had to ask. There were many a time we made a mistake. You'd cut it behind the poor woman's back and put it right. Or somebody would put it right for us. Somebody more experienced.
>
> 'We worked for Northern Trawlers and there was like benches each side and there must have been about forty people in this place. They used to have sing-songs and that, and the radio on for *Workers Playtime* at ten o'clock every morning. Oh yeah we used to sing and the older ones used to learn us the old songs. We had some good times. As I say it was hard on your hands and it was hard work. And I can remember the floor-woman coming into the toilets one day and saying to someone about me, "You know she's not gonna make a braider. I'm sure she's not gonna make a braider – she hasn't got the strength to do it." But I wouldn't give in. I didn't give in.

Braiders at Cosalt and Tanning

> 'I think at one time braiders had a bad name. You did if you worked on the dock. Well they just thought it was a lowly job and you must be the

same, but they were all decent women.'

As the industry declined and mechanisation made the job of net-braiding for fishing industry uses almost obsolete, Merle Boyington carried on working. She is one of the last net-braiders in Grimsby.

'It all came about when I was fifteen. A lady who lived opposite, she braided at home and asked why didn't I try it, and she let me have a go. And I liked doing things with my hands, sewing and knitting, to me that's what braiding is, like knitting, backwards and forwards. So then I went to Cosalt and Tanning and learned how to fill needles. You'd have three, four, five and six braiders you'd go round and fill for ten minutes. Then every so often they'd let you have a go on their net and show you how to braid. It was all women braiding, some down the dock, but there were lots doing it at home when their husbands were at sea. It meant I was here when my children came home from school and my husband worked shifts, so I could start when I liked as long as I got the work done. The wages weren't much. Depending on the size of the nets, it was six or seven pounds. We used to work from half-seven in the morning until five at night. Even the materials are different now; it was sisal twine in those days, so you used to get splinters in your hands and they would be red raw. At night when I got home I used to take all the splinters out and get a bottle of methylated spirit and put my hands in to harden the skin. Some of the braiders said to wee on them to harden the skin, but I used methylated spirit. You never used to be without a reel of prestaband. It was like a plastic plaster you would wind round your fingers. It was the only thing that wouldn't come off. At the factory, you were sat along beams and there were people the other side. I was there until I had my daughter when I was twenty-three. Then I didn't do any more until after I'd had my son and someone suggested I go to Middleton's down

Merle (right) teaching local residents to braid to raise money for the Fishermen's Memorial in 1996

the dock. So I went for an interview and the following Wednesday, they fetched me a net. They collect them Wednesday to Wednesday, one a week. I've been doing that for Middleton's for nearly thirty-eight years.

'I've done nets for all over the place, for oil tankers and the Humber Bridge when they were building that, for a circus, which had to be a circle. I did one a bit back for Hull football stadium. The most unusual one was for bats to stop them flying into cables. I did nearly fifty nets for the national grid. I did nets for the Oriana and the QE2 cruise ships to go over the swimming pools, another one was for the post office in Ipswich - that was a thousand and fifty-six rows and it had to be in one piece. If I do something unusual or big, I like to know what it's for, or where it's going.

'I got into the safety work when the fishing industry finished, it was a bit of a fluke. They used to do camouflage nets and they thought they'd try it and it took off. It's given Middleton's a living. They do a lot for the oil rigs, the helicopter nets – I can't do that heavy stuff. Some of the nets they do by machine, but some they want hand-braided because it's stronger, especially if they need a specific shape. If they cut it, it takes the strength out of it. There are only three of us now who do this. When I first started they had over eight-hundred braiders. It used to take them two days going round with the lorry. It'll be a shame when the skill dies out and it will eventually.'

Merle's net-braiding is as close as most women came to work at sea. For a few, that wasn't close enough. As long as she could remember, Mary-Rose Jessop had seen lads coming in from sea and found herself fascinated by their stories. She'd been pleasure tripping with her father, a skipper, but fishing had always been regarded as men's work. Then, after a spell without a job, her husband Charlie, mate on a seine netter, suggested she go to sea.

'It was something I'd always wanted to do. Out there you had no troubles, apart from your job if something went wrong, which sometimes it did. You got away from all the yapping. I've got books and books of photographs that I've taken. One time it was sparkling like a mill pond. And as you're gutting you throw the guts in the air and the seagulls come and dive down.

'First Charlie taught me the hard way to do things. I would fall asleep in my dinner I was that tired. Sometimes you're up in summer at three/four in the morning, you're lucky if you get to bed at two. I was just decky-cook then. We came in from sea and Charlie said, "What percentage is she on?" They gave me a hundred pounds and I was quite happy with that.

'The first trip I had no sea gear, so I had to borrow Charlie's. I looked like a little penguin, the sleeves was out here so I folded them all up. I couldn't wear the gloves 'cos they was massive and you can't gut like that. So I came in from sea and me hands was ripped to pieces 'cos I hadn't been wearing gloves and me dad says, "Oh my God." I said, "Dad what am I gonna do?" They was swollen and they was hurting, and he said, "Piss on 'em."'

Mary-Rose on board the deck of a seine netter

Mary-Rose wasn't the only woman at sea, but she wasn't always welcomed by men or other women.

'At sea everybody was laughing at me 'cos my hair was right down my back, and before I went on the deck. I used to put face cream on and do my hair and they used to say, "Where do you think you're going?" I said, "I always do this every morning, shut up." Two hours later I'd got mud and guts in my hair.

'The blokes'd shout, "Here comes the decky." And this bloke Johnny said, "Decky? She's just a woman. Charlie's only taking her to sea to..." I turned and I looked at him and I said, "Do you think so?" And he said, "She's doing a good bloke out of a job." I said to Charlie, "Sack me now and give him my job. I'll have the trip off." He got as far as Spurn Point, wouldn't do anything. They fetched him back, sacked him. I saw him after that I said, "Who's doing a good bloke out of a job?" He couldn't even make a cup of tea.

> 'There was one trip, we was twenty-eight days at sea, came in and landed four-hundred pounds in debt. See, you have to buy your own ice, your own oil, your own food everything, and that's between the crew. So we said, "We'll have a quick turnaround." Seven days dock to dock we made it and picked up a fortune. Of course, I took my dad out, suited up for him. He thought he was back at sea again. He was proud of me, at first he was mad because he'd had me privately educated, "From secretary to flaming fisherwoman." I said, "Dad I love it, it was your idea to be a secretary - I didn't want to be a secretary." I could never be a lady if I tried.'

Going to sea alongside husband Charlie didn't always work out, especially when the relationship was going through a difficult time.

> 'There was one trip when it was thick fog and it was freezing, I mean really freezing. You weren't man and wife at sea, that wouldn't have worked. We weren't getting on that well but we still sailed together even if we'd got our differences, but he'd started to take it out on me a bit. He told me to get forward and look for the buoy. It was a thick mist and I thought, *well it's got this metal thing on it you could have picked it up on the radar.* But he was the mate and I was the decky-cook. I did as I was told and that's it. So I stood there and stood there and it was that cold me nose started running and it turned into an icicle. We found the buoy in the end and I went to grab it and as I did it hit me across my eye and it was bleeding, but of course you have to jump over the deck boards to get to the other side to clip it up otherwise you've been steaming all that time for nothing. All me nets would have gone, the lot. I always did what I was told, that's what I was there for. I've got this scar over my eye to show for it.'

Alison Josefsen first went to sea at the age of 18 on her father's seine netter. Covering for her brother Ejnar who'd broken his leg in a motorbike accident, her first trip lasted 22 days.

> 'Dad was short handed and I was unemployed at the time and he says to me, "Why don't you come?" With me dad being a skipper I slept in the wheel house, he had a portaloo for me. And I didn't go sleep where the men were. But my uncle was on board the boat, then me dad and then just Phil. He was married but he knew me anyway. We was coming up near Spurn Point on the way back and me Dad says, "Well are you coming back?" I went, "Oh yeah." And me grandfather and me uncles,

Allison Josefsen at work

everyone, they were so proud of me.

'Of course I got some shit. I got accused of sleeping with my dad and everything. Just people with sick minds. I did a job. That was my job. That's when I moved up north and there were some really nasty people. The women were absolutely horrendous. I got a bit sick of it in the end. But when we were trawling, which I loved, you used to start about three or four in the morning, sometimes you could get done at midnight. It all depended on how much you caught for the day. It was like that prawning at Christmas time, so you was in at night each night and sometimes you'd get finished and you'd just pop for a pint on the way home or sometimes I didn't even go home and I just slept aboard the boat. 'Cos some days you was just absolutely shattered.'

Like Mary-Rose Jessop, Allison was signed on as a decky-cook.

'That meant I did all the cooking, and then when they were busy I did the same as the men basically. I took me watch. Although it was a bit frightening sometimes I will admit that. It usually worked out I'd go on the first watch or whatever and me dad would be in my bunk so if there was any complications I'd just have to shout me dad. Couple of years down the line what used to frighten me was walking from the wheel house down to the cabins to wake the next person up. You used to put the kettle on for 'em and I used to think, *God if I went over board no one would know would they? We're steaming to the next fishing ground and if I tripped...*

'The fishermen, they were fine. They used to give me cheek. I used to be one step ahead of 'em all the time. When I moved up north with my parents, we was well known 'cos ours was a fishing family. It was mainly like when you go out in the pub, say like you'd be home for the weekend or it was bad weather. And I never had no friends, all I had was my mum, my dad, my brothers and sisters so when I used to go out I used to be one of the lads. I used to drink with the lads off the boat, the lads off the quay. They just treated me like one of them. And then of course you get some with girlfriends and they've never met me or vice versa and that's when a lot of it started, just vicious rumours.'

Falling out with her father on one occasion resulted in Allison being sacked, but it wasn't about to prevent her from going to sea, and making a point to her father.

'My friend's husband let me go on his boat. Well my dad see his arse didn't he? He didn't think I'd be able to get a job on another boat. And I just thought, *no, I'll show you.* I just helped out, you know when me friend's husband was short for crew and that. 'Cos you'd go down at say three or four in the morning and all the boats were trying to get out and then you got some that are just rolling out the pub or whatever. So a lot of 'em didn't used to turn up.'

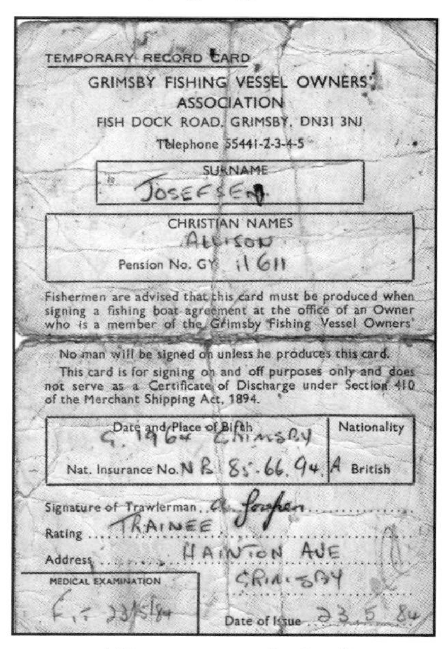

TEMPORARY RECORD CARD

GRIMSBY FISHING VESSEL OWNERS' ASSOCIATION

FISH DOCK ROAD, GRIMSBY, DN31 3NJ

Telephone 55441-2-3-4-5

SURNAME JOSEFSEN

CHRISTIAN NAMES ALLISON

Pension No. GY 11611

Fishermen are advised that this card must be produced when signing a fishing boat agreement at the office of an Owner who is a member of the Grimsby Fishing Vessel Owners'

No man will be signed on unless he produces this card.

This card is for signing on and off purposes only and does not serve as a Certificate of Discharge under Section 410 of the Merchant Shipping Act, 1894.

Date and Place of Birth 9. 1964 GRIMSBY

Nat. Insurance No. NB 85.66.94.A

Nationality British

Signature of Trawlerman

Rating TRAINEE

Address HAINTON AVE GRIMSBY

MEDICAL EXAMINATION FIT 23/5/84

Date of Issue 23.5.84

Allison was one of only a few women who were officially signed on a ship

The dangers of the sea were brought home on one trip when her father had gone to help another ship in trouble.

'They'd broken down in really bad weather. The waves were bigger than this house and you're just bobbing up and down and round and round, and all you can see is the tops of the white waves. I've never seen lightning like it in my life. I was laid in my bunk in the sleeping bag, thinking, *if I'm gonna die, I'm gonna die under here.* But me dad knew we were okay, he said to me when we got back into dock, "Allison if we'd have been in trouble you would have been up there in the helicopter." I said, "You wouldn't 'ave got me up there." But they'd knock you out anyway before they take you up. Honestly if you'd have seen them, just dangling... Oh God – I'll never forget it until the day I die.

'I wasn't on a percentage like the other crew. So I'd get so much a trip.

And then when we moved up north I did go on a percentage, but I was like on three percent and they was all on a lot more than me. But I mean I've got a good dad he's always looked after me. Still looks after me today. You could earn some really good money and then sometimes you could come in and you wouldn't have a penny. My mam, she used to go down and every week her wages was there. Well you think about it, dad hadn't even put a fish in the net. So like when you come in from sea you've got all the food to buy, all the diesel, all the ice everything. So after everything's been taken out of that, sometimes you'd be lucky to pick twenty pounds up. That's what I say about a hard life. Yeah the miners… but they still had a wage each week, whereas in the fishing industry, if you didn't catch a fish you didn't eat.'

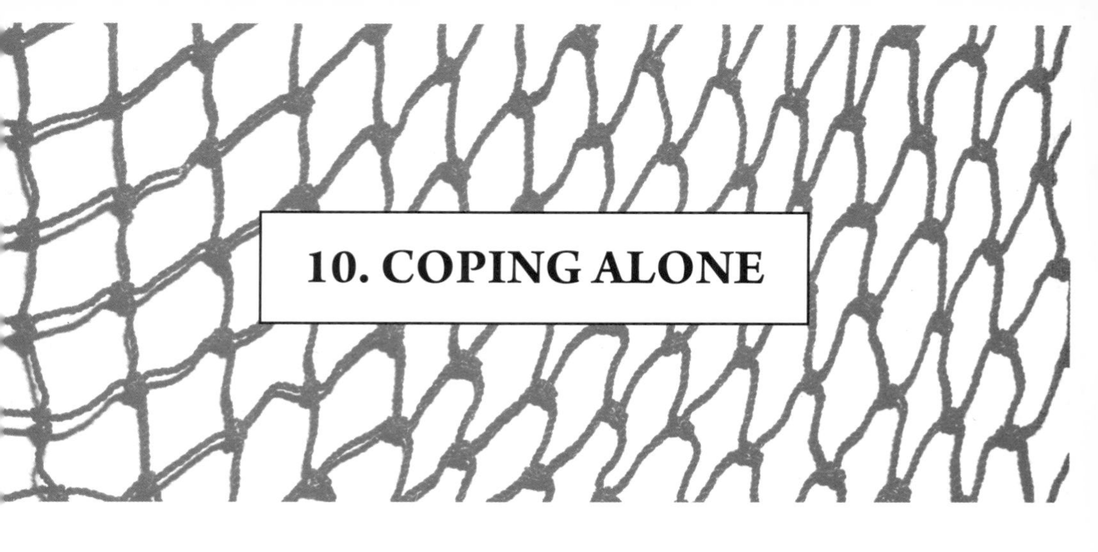

10. COPING ALONE

'He never thought to say, how did you manage? He just took it for granted that you would.'

The stresses of an often isolated existence affected women in different ways. Sally Wilbourne had managed well and hadn't been aware of the influence her husband's absences at sea had been having until her health began to suffer.

> 'I had a mild heart attack. They put it down to stress, you know – and I was in intensive care and they were saying, I shouldn't do this and I shouldn't do that. And I'm a person that likes to be on the go. I became so depressed. Actually my girls paid for me to have a private consultation in Hull. The consultant said to me, "Providing that you don't do anything excessive, you can live a long life. The heart attack was a warning." He said, "The biggest problem with you is stress - you take too much to heart at times and the biggest problem is the stress from your husband actually." I hadn't thought I was bothered by it all but obviously I was. And being so on my own and not having anyone that I could talk things over with and everything. I mean it was a long time to be doing this.'

Originally from Sunderland, Sally had found it difficult to develop close relationships within the tight knit fishing community.

> 'I lost a child while Tom was at sea. I developed high blood pressure and I was taken into Croft Baker and I lost the baby. There was nothing wrong

with him, a fully formed little boy apparently, but the blood pressure of course you know. And Tom wasn't here so I was sort of on my own with that.

'If I'd been living in Sunderland I would have had… people weren't nosy or anything but they were there for you. I was in this house for three days and nobody even came to see how I was or whether I was around or anything. That's when I got upset. The fact that I lived here and I knew them, but they all seemed to be so busy getting on with their own lives. There were lots of times I could have done with Tom's help.

Sally with daughters Helen and Andrea

'One time Helen had pneumonia and my doctor hardly ever left the house. He used to say, "Oh I'm worried for her." Times like that I could have done with having him around you know just to back me up. And it might have been better if I'd had family in the town, someone to talk to or to come round and see me, but I did have to battle on with it, without him there. And of course by the time he came home most things were right again. He never thought to say, how did you manage? He just took it for granted that you would. But I think that was the same for most fisherman's wives, we just did it.'

Angela McMullen's mother was another who found the solitary life of a fisherman's wife hard to come to terms with, particularly in the early years of her marriage.

'She couldn't cope with the drink. She'd never come across it. The way she was brought up was pretty prim and proper and coming into Grimsby it was completely different. None of the neighbours had husbands that went to sea in Yarborough Road. My mother befriended the wireless operator's wife, then her whole life changed. We went with them when they went down Freeman Street, or into Franklins for a meal. Once me mother started to go out with me father, they went out the four of them together, then she felt more part of it, but before then when he was drinking we didn't know where he was. I can remember praying for me father to come home. It was pretty fraught for me mother cause she hadn't a clue. We didn't have a car. We didn't have money for going around finding out where they were. But yes in the early days she said she'd have put her head in the gas oven if it hadn't have been for us three.'

The Jones', Angela (middle bottom) with her family

For some women, especially those with large families, responsibility fell to the older children to help bring up the younger ones and fill the gap made by absent fathers. Extended family networks were often the difference between coping and not coping. Mike Connor was brought up by the women in his family.

'Me father, me grandfather, they was at sea for three weeks at a time and only used to get two days in dock. One day he used to take my mother out - that was her reward for bringing up eight children - one day out at the Clee Park Club which used to be near Ramsdens. Me auntie and me granny used to look after us. The women, they'd all rally round and help each other. I was the eldest so I used to help me mother. Every Saturday we used to go down to the market and I used to help at Christmas. I had to be the father figure 'cos me dad was never there. And even when he came in dock you didn't see him because he just wanted to go for a drink. After three weeks at sea he didn't understand - he used to take us to Nobles and buy us a Walls ice cream. And that was it. My mother took it in her stride. She was brought up in a fishing family so she accepted it you see - like I did.

'Mrs Cox down our street, she had seventeen children and it was known she looked after them and kept them in line while her husband was at sea the whole time. She had the record down Taylor Street, I thought we had plenty but seventeen's not bad is it? She had that many kids that if they was playing up you had to get out the way; she'd come into the back passage and you'd all get a smack - she had that many she couldn't remember which was hers. They had a round bed and the kids all slept with their feet in the middle, you know in a circle.'

Mrs Cox wasn't the only woman with a large family whose sense of community extended to other children in the neighbourhood. Pete Woods remembers Sylvie Hargreaves as a second mother.

> 'She had about ten kids and old Albert her husband was a fisherman. Frank, Alfie, Dave – all the sons was fishermen. Whenever I was hungry I'd go to Sylvie's. Sylvie was everybody's mum. She was hard as nails believe me; she'd knock you out if you give her any lip. There was mother May and father Louis, they were another pair where if you was hungry you'd go to them. They had an open door. I had times where I didn't have nowt to put on me feet when I was a kid. But Sylvie she had ten kids and five sons and if I was round there with Dave, whatever Dave dunt want anymore, I'd have that. I was actually walking round like a fisherman when I was twelve, in the gear. 'Cos that's what they do, they gave it to the younger ones.'

Marjorie Louis invented a novel way of keeping her children in check on their father's long absences. Her daughter Lorraine remembers, it was her three brothers who tried their mother's patience.

> 'We had an old deck, a tape recorder you know with the reels of tape. Me mam used to say, "Right, now I'm putting the tape recorder on and I'm recording what you've done for your father, then when he gets home he can sort you out." And she used to play the tape back to him when we'd been naughty and say, "Listen to what I've had to put up with," and then we'd get in trouble.'

A night out at the bingo was an integral part of many women's social life. It offered the chance to meet other women and, as Marjorie discovered, there was always the chance you'd strike it lucky.

> I went to the Rialto and I won ninety-nine pounds. When I gets home, George is laid out on the settee watching telly and he asked if I'd done any good. I took all the money from this envelope and I just shook it over him, and he said, what was I going to do with it? And I said, "Take driving lessons." So I took me driving lessons and passed my test second time. I got my own car, an Austin Cambridge. That was my first car, it was lovely, a really old fashioned thing.'

Although it was impossible to maintain conventional family ties, fishermen at sea would often send telegrams for special occasions. For women like Doreen Tyson, her father's messages are treasured possessions, a reminder that they were not forgotten.

> 'I've got a telegram here from the day I got married, as he was at sea – I think we all got married when he was away. My brother had to give me away. He had to go if he got a ship. And because you didn't have telephones in those days, they'd send a telegram. When he was at sea we used to have a special radio you could tune into the fishing wave band – the one the fisherman used to communicate with each other via the ship's radio. We were able to tune into this and every night round about the same time, if he wasn't busy, he would come on and talk to us on this radio, we could listen to him … and he had his own personal call sign so that we knew he was calling to us. He used to come on and say, "Piccolo, piccolo, piccolo Pete. Piccolo, piccolo, piccolo…" and he'd do that for a few minutes and then we knew that what he was going to say was for us. We couldn't reply to him or anything so I mean it was just one way of communication.'

Deslys Fairfield remembers her disappointment that her father hadn't been able to make it home for her wedding.

> 'The ship was running late. He must have been deep sea and I think they'd got bad weather. He sent me a telegram, because he knew he wasn't gonna get back. He missed me wedding and me granddad had to give me away, at the last minute more or less. I think he only missed it by about two days. I had to get all dressed up in my wedding gown and everything to show me dad when he come in. But it's not the same. Nothing's the same if it doesn't happen on the day.

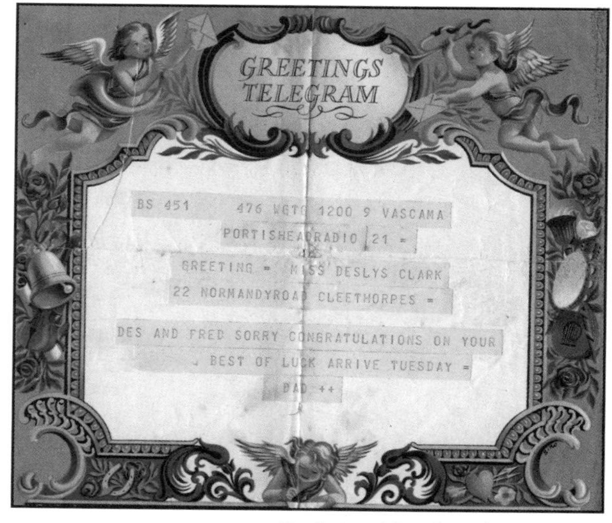

GREETINGS TELEGRAM

BS 451 476 WGTG 1200 9 VASCAMA
PORTISHEADRADIO 21 =
GREETING = MISS DESLYS CLARK
22 NORMANDYROAD CLEETHORPES =
DES AND FRED SORRY CONGRATULATIONS ON YOUR
BEST OF LUCK ARRIVE TUESDAY =
DAD ++

Deslys' wedding day telegram

> 'Once your father works away you don't think of him not being there,

> only on really important occasions like a wedding. Mine was the most important thing I think he missed regards a big occasion. I think he was home for all the other weddings. Yeah, mine was the only wedding he missed I think.'

As Margaret Monger remembers, for her mother it was understood that marrying into the fishing life would mean coping with her husband's absence.

> 'Maybe she missed him now and again, but it was never obvious to us. She ran everything anyway and having four daughters...we were a handful, we got up to mischief as most kids. When we moved here, mum used to be gardening after we went to bed, me and my next youngest sister – she's only eighteen months younger than me – we used to creep out of bed and sit with our elbows on the windowsill watching her and she'd say, "Get back into bed." But we just used to bob down and get up again.'

Josephine Gibney is keen to set the record straight on the way fishermen's wives have been given a bad press.

> 'I've been writing articles about "fishwives". I'm sick of hearing that, seeing pictures of women with their hair in curlers, a cigarette in their mouth – fish-wife. *Oh they've got a mouth like a fish-wife.* It gets me goat but the point is we're not all like that.'

Although as Josephine, for many years a magistrate in Grimsby points out, for some women coping alone wasn't strictly above board.

> 'If Frank's gone that morning tide, I've seen them, one chap going into another's house before they're even out of the lock pit. They've got their fancy man in. A lot of 'em had it. When I was down King Edward Street, I used to say to me mother, "Mam why's Mrs so and so put that lamp or that vase with a flower in the front room like that?" She'd tell me I didn't wanna know. But I found out it meant the hubby was just coming in or he'd just gone out and it was a message. You learnt it all growing up.'

Looking back, former fisherman Pete Woods is able to view objectively the speed with which he and his wife, and many other couples, met and married. In many cases, young women found themselves married and alone after a whirlwind courtship.

> 'I met Janice on the afternoon, I sailed at two o'clock in the morning,

came in the next trip, met her again then moved in with her. I'd known her for twenty-four hours. But that's the way it was, you didn't have time to go through a year's courting. If you did it over a year, it's still only sixty or seventy hours a month. The best thing about having somebody was you had someone to come home to. It's horrible coming home when you didn't have anyone to come home to. So maybe some people got into it for the wrong reason.

'I never really looked at it from the wives' point of view – maybe because like most deckies when I came home I was too pissed to care – but we got caught in a storm once and we were missing for five days. We lost all the aerials and so couldn't radio, it's a hurricane; there's no ships. So we were just dodging and bashing through this hurricane. When the storm eased down they climbed up on top of the bridge and we managed to connect some wires, and we managed to get the black box working and called up another ship and then they relayed it back here. And my ex-wife had been staying at the skipper's house because the skipper I was with at the time he used to radio home to his missus every day and of course there was no calls. So she went to the office and said, "Look I haven't heard from him what's going on?" After five days, the ship was pretty badly damaged. When I came home that's probably the only time I saw that side of my ex-wife, because she really did think we'd gone.

'If I'd have been a fisherman's wife there's no way I could sit at home for ten and a half months a year not knowing if he's alive, dead, knowing that when he came home more than likely he'd be pissed all the time. They had to have another life; they needed it for their sanity. I mean some fishermen were violent, when they came home they'd think nowt of beating the crap out of the wife. I've seen too much of that. So sometimes when the wife knows what's coming home, you know maybe they don't really want them home. Maybe she wants to be with that person at the beginning but a lot of fishermen's marriages were done too fast.'

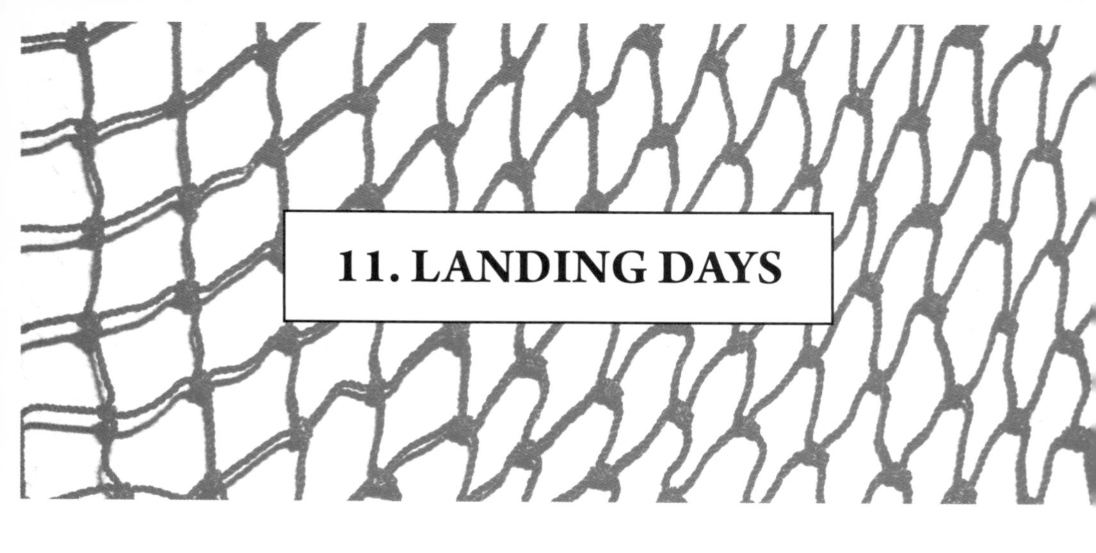

11. LANDING DAYS

'... a big tin of Quality Street.'

On the day the ship came home, if the catch had been good there would be money – presuming it didn't find its way from a fisherman's pocket to a Freeman Street pub. For many women, making sure at least some of their husband's settlings found their way into the family kitty was the first priority. It wasn't always an amenable homecoming; there were usually police on the dockside. For the lucky ones there was a sense of anticipation. Olga Drever made sure she always met husband Steve, and one particular ship holds a fond place in her memory.

> '*Ashanti* – I never missed meeting Steve on that ship. It was such a happy ship and if they came in at evening time - they'd made a recording of that song – *It's only a Shanty in Old Shanty Town*. And as soon as they came through the lock gates, they'd play it from the bridge. Another time they pulled me aboard at the lock gate and I came in on the bow, standing with the mate as the ship came in. And someone shouted from the dock, "That's the finest mate I've seen in along time." You had laughs and you had sad times. When we bought our house we called it *Ashanti* and when we moved we took the name plaque. My son kept it and when he married and bought his first house in Cape Town, he called it *Ashanti* and now he lives in Chicago and his house there is called *Ashanti*.'

Often, landing day offered husbands and wives the only chance to spend a day together. Women, whose social opportunities were few, looked forward to a night on the town. But as Ann Graves remembers, there were times her husband would know the catch had been bad.

> 'He used to come home on landing day and we were supposed to be going out. He'd say, "We'd better stay in 'cos I don't think we've done very good. I'll run round the corner to the phone box." And you knew when he come back whether you'd dress up like a skipper's wife to go out for the day, or put the kids in a push-chair and go to the park – you never usually took your kids with you landing day that was your day together. Many a time he's come back and said, "We better go to the park." I'd say, "How much do you owe them?" If you land in debt, you owe the gaffers money so you have to pay that from the next trip's money. That happened more than not, but when we did make what you would call a killing, if you made seven or eight thousand pounds – we were millionaires! They used to be called two day millionaires and anybody could have it, anybody that was out of a ship could have a couple of quid. Anything I needed I could have it. Have a new dress every trip and then when the kids come, he'd buy 'em two toys because he couldn't make his mind up which to buy. There wasn't many of them that wasn't daft with money and they'd give away all they earned. And the old bums and a lot of young bums used to be stood round Riby Street and Riby Square waiting for a 'Wesley'- that was what they called the fishermen that was earning – and they'd stand there waiting and it'd be, "Here, c'mon I'll take you for a couple of pints." If they managed to get away without you on a landing day, by the time they got home these bums ended up with more of your husband's money than you got! That's the way it was done. And it was accepted, part of a way of life. Ooh I hated 'em. I'd think, *get yourself off to bloody sea, my old man's got to go.* That's why there wasn't many landing days he got out without me.'

Despite Ann's best efforts, there were occasions Graham found his way to the pub.

> 'He'd gone out. I can't remember why I hadn't gone, whether I couldn't get a babysitter or what, but he was coming straight back. He said, "Get Zane ready."
>
> 'I can't remember what I had on, but my little boy he had a beautiful green double breasted coat with a little velvet collar and he was a proper ginger-nut my lad, lovely thick auburn hair. And we waited and waited for

Graham coming back to get us. I thought, *I'm not having this.* So I got the money off my father and took a taxi into town and I went in every pub down Freeman Street, storming in like a battleship. I thought, *I will find you.* And apparently, he'd go in, say, The Corporation and I'd be across at The Angel. And they'd say, "Eh Graham, your old woman's just been in here with your lad. You better keep out the way 'cos she's steaming." And he said afterwards, "I went in three or four and I thought I'd better keep out of the way." So he went in The White Bear and it was the first day that it opened and you couldn't get in the door. It was that packed I couldn't get in, so he hid and I never found him. I can laugh about it now but at the time I'd have cheerfully strangled him myself.

'I remember one day he'd gone out and he was ages, you know. I'm looking out the bay window at the front and the taxi come round the corner and out he fell. And as he staggered in the back gate he had a bloody great big yellow duck under one arm – you know the ones the kids used to sit along and push – and under this arm he had like a racing car that they sat on and pushed. He couldn't make his mind up which of these two things to buy for our little one, our boy, so he bought 'em both. I remember as if it was yesterday looking at him as he was staggering in the gate. "I'm late darling!" He said. And I went in and took his cold dinner from the work surface and as he got to the back door I let it go, and he ducked – of course he was that drunk – he fell backwards. A couple of hours later there's a little tap on my back kitchen window and it was a little old woman lived next door to us then – and she said, "Are you all right Ann?" So I said, "Yes of course, why what's the matter?" She said, "Well I heard you shouting and screaming when Graham came home, and then we saw the dinner come out the back door." I said, "Oh yeah fine. He's on the settee in the front room, snoring his head off." And when he got up, it was like nothing had happened, you know it was done and finished.'

Emma Brennan had her own way of dealing with a few too many pints on landing day; a trick passed down from mother to daughter.

'When he used to come home and he'd had a drink, he'd fall asleep in the chair. He'd wake up having had nothing to eat all day and say he was hungry. So I used to put bacon fat round his lips when he was asleep. I'd say, "You've already eaten. I'm doing no more." I wasn't waiting while he sobered up to cook his meal if he wasn't here to get it. And the kids used to howl with laughter. He'd say, "Is that right kids? Have I had me dinner?" They'd say, "Yes dad, yeah you've eaten your bacon." I learnt that from me mother. She used to say, "Wipe the bacon round, he'll never know the difference." He wasn't ever what you would call a boozer though. He was more for his kids. He used to carry them shoulder high each one, the two boys Mark and Robert. He loved them kids, adored them. He'd push the pram, he'd do anything, and you didn't see many men pushing prams in them days. He did. He wasn't bothered about looking daft pushing a pram. "Go on," I'd say, "push the pram, they're your sons."'

Dennis Brennan, victim of 'the bacon fat trick'

For the children of fishermen, part of the attraction of landing day was a present from 'the bond'. Bonded goods were available to fishermen at duty-free prices. Although there are tales of skippers adding a little extra to the price of bonded goods by way of an unofficial gratuity. If the tide was right, Rita Whittle would meet her husband on landing days.

> 'We'd have the same taxi driver to take us down to the lockpits and then follow them round until they tied up on the pontoon. I know my kids remember that when he came in from sea he'd have his bond and he'd always have a medium sized tin of Quality Street. That was what the kids looked forward to – he always bought them something out the bond, especially if he'd been away at Christmas.'

As Doreen Tyson remembers the bond wasn't all her father brought home.

> 'They used to take stuff on the trawlers, probably drink as well. In fact I'm sure they took drink and chocolate, and it was sealed and they couldn't use it until later when they'd got to the three mile limit or whatever. I don't know how it worked but he used to often come in with tins of Quality Street. Never used to bring booze in, he'd probably drunk it.

'He always had two or three big basses of fish, fresh fish and lobster still alive. Unfortunately we didn't have freezers in those days so we had to give a lot away. We'd often open the pantry and there'd be a couple of lobsters on the pantry floor. But my mother, she could gut fish, scale it, clean crab, dress crabs, lobsters and everything.'

Marjorie Louis and her daughter, Lorraine, remember homecomings and the ubiquitous tin of Quality Street for different reasons.

Marjorie:

'He always sent me a bouquet when he was coming in the river and the neighbours used to say, "Eh up, Madge has got George coming home, she's cleaning the windows." And you did, everything had to be spick and span – your husband's coming home! He always brought back this big tin of Quality Street. Well in them days you only got them if you were a fisherman, from the bond shop.'

Lorraine:

'We used to think, *Dad's coming in, we can have Quality Street*. He'd come in, put the tin down and say, "Sit down there kids, enjoy!" I'll always remember being sat with this Quality Street tin, all four of us, no mam and dad. We used to sit eating these sweets. We thought it was absolutely brilliant. There was toffee on the carpet, and we'd just finished eating these chocolates and then from upstairs came mam and dad.'

Marjorie:

'They wondered where we'd gone. I won't tell you no more!'

Rita Whittle's husband, George, was one of few fishermen who took time away from the sea, spending a year doing factory work. The adjustment to life ashore was difficult for both of them and old habits were hard to break.

> 'The drink was a problem for me. I could have been in a much better position if it wasn't for the drink. A lot was pissed up the wall. Even when he packed in, he still liked his drink. I'm looking at these Jeremy Kyle programmes and if it was this day and age he'd have been alcohol dependant, a lot of them were. He didn't get on with factory work. It was too much of a routine. Plus, I didn't like it, because I was the Missis of the house when he was away and when he was here, I wasn't. It was a little old-fashioned maybe, but you were a bit more under the thumb. I was the Missis for three weeks, then he'd come home for three or four days, I could cope with that, or having a week on holiday, somewhere different. You were at their beck and call, but I felt you had to make up for them being away.'

Margaret Monger's father's homecoming routine saw him spending time with his family.

> 'We were always let off school and my mum and dad'd pick us up, me first as the eldest, and we used to go out to my grandma's. We'd spend the time out there until, maybe seven o'clock. Then we'd come home and go to bed and he'd probably be sailing on the afternoon tide the next day. So I saw very little of him. I worked out that up until 1939 when the war broke out, the most we used to see him was fourteen days a year. My dad wasn't a typical fisherman. He didn't drink, he didn't swear - I can honestly say I didn't hear him say as much as damn, ever - certainly not in front of his family. I gather from my uncles he could hold his own. Well, he wouldn't be a skipper if he didn't hold his own.
>
> 'We never went to see him at the docks when he came in. I know a lot of wives who did go down the docks when the ship came in. I know my aunt used to go down and see him but mum never did. She used to stand at the gate; the taxi would pick him up. She used to wait until he was out of sight at Fiveways and that was it. It was felt that if you went down to see your husband off or see him come in, there was a feeling that you didn't trust him because of what he might get up to.'

As a child, Deslys Fairfield was used to her father being away being part of his job;

although like many fishermen, he left his work at sea when he came home.

'He never really told us a lot of stories. I also remember once when I wasn't very well – I used to have a lot of septic throats as a kid – anyway I wasn't very well and me dad had come in and he'd been to Greenland. I can remember him saying about the white polar bears and he said, "There was one with her little babies." I says, "Ooh did you bring one home dad?" And he said, "Yeah, go get one out my kitbag." But he was only joking you know, things like that he'd say. If he saw something spectacular, he'd tell you. He fished a lot in Iceland and he used to say the fjords were beautiful.'

HIGH WATER

JUNE		a.m.	p.m.
Fri.	6	4.50	5. 9
Sat.	7	5.32	5.55

FISH DOCKS

ARRIVALS: THURSDAY, P.M., Royal Marine, Erillus, Vilda, Stafnes, Konsul Dubbers (German), Novelli, Kingston Onyx (Hullman), Dona (Dane).—Friday, A.M., Recono, Arabis, Emmi, Imperia, Franken (German), Jenny Ronn (Dane).

SAILINGS: THURSDAY, P.M., Flensburg (German), Walter Siemers (German), Hanne Bjerrigaard (Dane), Sinne Bjerrigaard (Dane).—FRIDAY, A.M., Erillus, Flying Wing, Peken, Claire, Tunisian, Rose of England, R[illegible]co, Libyan, Trevani, Malayan, Chrysolite, Onward, Macedonian, Remindo, Novelli.

ROYAL DOCK

ARRIVALS: THURSDAY, P.M., nil.—FRIDAY, A.M., nil.

SAILINGS: THURSDAY, P.M., Havny (Finnish), 662 (F. Bengtsson), Abo, coal; Harry Richardson (British), 1,198 (Arthur Cook), London, coal.—FRIDAY, A.M., Grampian Coast (British), 258 (Moffat and Craigie), Hull, general r.o.b.

SHIPS IN DOCK: Discharging at 9.30 a.m. Loading: Tora Elise (coke), Erna Ronnebaum (coal). Repairs: Bridlington, Belray, R.F.A. King Salvor, H.M.S. Jewel.

IMMINGHAM

ARRIVALS: THURSDAY, P.M., Oranus (Norwegian), 6,195 (W. Moran), Thameshaven, oil; Lord Citrine (British), 1,762 (Arthur Cook), London, light; Cormarsh (British), 1,652 (Arthur Cook), London, light; Brandaris (Dutch), 115 (T. E. Kettlewell), Goole, light; Evita Swedish), 825 (Arthur Cook), Rochester, light; Tyreso (Swedish), 2,243 (F. Bengtsson), Middlesbrough, light; Leadsman (British), 220 (J. R. Rix), Sunderland, light.—FRIDAY, A.M., nil.

SAILINGS: THURSDAY, P.M., Rehhorst (German), 756 (Lambert Bros.), Copenhagen, coalite, Barford (British), 1,763 (Arthur Cook), Ipswich, coal Heluan (German), 855 (John Good), Aalborg, coal.—FRIDAY, A.M., Oranus (Norwegian), 6,195 (W. Moran), Rotterdam, light; Heyshott (British), 1,586 (Arthur Cook), London, coal.

SHIPS IN DOCK: Discharging at 9.30 a.m. Charles M (phosphates). Loading: Scandia, Pinewood, Hugo Oldendorff, [illegible]wcombe (coal), Leadsman (spirit). Waiting berth: Hudson Sound, Concordia, Rogate, Lord Citrine, Cormarsh, Brandaris, Evita, Tyreso (coal). Repairs: Cable Enterprise, Hodder, Vestal, Gold Ranger, Vienna, H.M.S. Ariadne, Robert Middleton, Roman Queen.

The *Grimsby Evening Telegraph*: ships' arrivals and catches

As engineer for 13 years, Angela McMullen's father was the longest serving member on the trawler *The Churchill.* On the return trip, he'd send a telegram telling them which tide the ship was on; this would give her mother time to make preparations for his return.

'We always looked in the paper to see how many kit the ship had made. And my mother and I would go down dock to meet him. As soon as I was old enough, when the telegram came I'd go down on my bike to the dock police and get a pass. 'Cos you couldn't go out on the dock without one. So that was my job. And then we would go down and wait on the swing bridge. There was a little watchman's hut there and he used to take pity on us because it was pretty cold down there sometimes late at night. We would go in there and then we would walk round to No1 fish dock and wait for the ship to berth. Sometimes I'd be climbing up on one ship, two ships, three ships to get to him. You know climbing on the fish boxes; if the tide was in they piled them high. My father was an Engineer and so he had to shut the engines down. We always had a big bake up and a clean up before he came in. That telegram was a signal to say - right, get the house cleaned and have a big bake up – mince pies, jam tarts anything like that. We

> would take them down because when they came in the dock there was no stores left on board and that's when they had a drink. And they would hit the whisky, drinking on an empty stomach. And so mam said, "Get some cakes into your father, try and keep him sober." The next morning he would be up, smart, down the dock to collect his settlings. Sometimes they were in debt, most of the time they had some money. Then after that they hit the pubs, they'd only probably had toast for breakfast. So that's where it went, some people spent a lot. Me father didn't spend a lot on drink but enough to come home in a taxi drunk. I remember him once getting out of a taxi and falling in the hedge. Another time he come in and he just passed out on the floor and I couldn't have been more than six and me mother put the play-pen round 'cos I had a younger sister. And she said, "Don't touch him, just leave him. Let him sober up." And when he sobered up we would have a full roast dinner, the works. It would be eight or nine o'clock at night and we'd be all sitting there having a Sunday dinner. By two o'clock the next morning he was gone for another three or three and a half weeks. And so it was back to just us and mother.'

While it is true that many fishermen earned their reputation as committed and excessive drinkers: the cycle of weeks of hard work in unforgiving conditions followed by two or three days ashore demanded a release of pressure for some men. Ann Graves is able to place her own experiences into perspective.

> 'I listened to stories with 'em all years ago, I've seen photographs where they're chipping ice away from the ship and I've talked to the men and lived with the man that did it. When yer waiting for them to come home, if they've gone for a couple of pints and they say they'll be back in a couple of hours, you know damn well they're not coming back - there's always somebody that they're gonna see and you get all het up about it. But when you think about it, there was no wonder. There's absolutely no wonder. It was a way of life.'

Pete Woods' time ashore frequently ended before a judge or magistrate. The often brutal realities of life at sea made the short transition to shore life a struggle.

> 'Usually landing day I got arrested for fighting or sleeping in Freeman Street or summat. And this judge had seen me for the about the seventh time in a year and he actually said to me, "You're not a criminal Mr Woods, just a nuisance. Why is it that you are always drunk when you're in dock?" And the only thing that came to me 'ead, but I suppose it was

> the truth really, I'd actually had a bad trip, a mate of mine had got lost on another ship. And a mate of mine on the ship I was on had got crushed. It didn't make me act any differently but… I just said to him I wanted to forget the trip I was just on and forget the fact I was going back in sixty hours and what better way to do it than stay drunk?'

For some families, the combination of drink and homecoming brought with it a difficult mix of emotions. Lydia Sinclair experienced the extremes of behaviour and destructive consequences of her father's years of excessive drinking.

> 'You didn't do anything to make him angry, because he was drunk from about twelve o'clock onwards, but not on the first night when he used to come home. My mother used to meet him, and then she used to go down the dock with him the next day to get his pay to stop him spending it in the pubs and gambling. Then they always went out together. My mother never drank to excess, but he always got drunk on those nights. He could never go out socially and not drink.
>
> 'I think you were always excited because your father was coming home. The bond, we never got any of that. I do remember boxes of chocolates, but they were for my mother, so we never ever got anything special when he came home from sea, not extra pocket money, nothing at all. We dreaded it, you're excited a bit but you dreaded it the rest of the time because you just kept out of his way. Meal times, he was just sitting down there falling drunk, at Christmas time as well. I look back and there was never a happy Christmas, because he used to get up in the morning, and the pubs opened earlier then, and in the two hours they were open he used to consume as much drink as he possibly could, come home, and you were sitting waiting to have Christmas dinner, and he was argumentative, nasty. So it was never happy, nobody got up on Christmas morning to have their presents. My twin brother and I got up and opened our presents; it was never anything to do with the family, basically because my mother was ground down.
>
> 'Mother never spoke about her history. She did these pictures when she was very young, but she never did anything like that in later life. She used to write when she was younger and had things published, she just gave up I think. They never had any friends. She just stayed at home. She knew the neighbours, but they weren't a big part of her life.

'He wasn't an alcoholic because he went on the trawlers; he was an alcoholic long before that. Even being a little girl I can remember certain things; he was drunk all his life. The sea drink was worse than when he was on shore, because it was so intensive. It was three days of real bingeing to the point where he had the DTs. I've seen him with the DTs and they've had to take him to hospital. He was in Reykjavik hospital for two or three weeks. It's unusual because when you go to sea you're not normally allowed a lot to drink; it's rationed. He said he wasn't drunk and he fell over the step, but it was a severe injury. Going to sea was an easy excuse to drink a lot more. I think he hated the hard work of it because he wasn't a young person. We were born when he was nearly forty, so it was in his fifties that he was actually having to go back to sea, and not the kind of sea that he'd left behind on the cruise liners. He told us he hated it, but in a way that made you feel it was your fault. He was the sort of person that never should have got married, and certainly never should have had children.'

12. HIGH DAYS AND HOLIDAYS

'... round Spurn and back again all for two shillings and sixpence...'

Finding time for family holidays was always difficult for fishermen. Time off was always precious and making arrangements in advance was virtually impossible. Taking a trip off meant a loss of earnings as well as the cost of the holiday. For the children growing up in fishing families, simple pleasures, parties, days out and breaks from routine were invariably provided by women. Although as Rita Whittle remembers, when husband George's ship was in dock for repair on one occasion, the family took full advantage.

> 'The ship had a breakdown and had to go on the slips for a fortnight. Andrew was only eighteen months old and George came in on a Wednesday, said we're going to be in dock a fortnight so we might as well go away. He gave me some money and I went up to the travel agent in Brighowgate and I booked a week to Butlins. This was the Wednesday and we went to Butlins on the Saturday. You had to do things on the spur of the moment.'

An offer of a trip to London in the *Grimsby Evening Telegraph* in 1969 gave George and Rita their first chance of a weekend away.

> 'The lady over the road said she'd look after my kids and we went to London. It was the first time George and I had been away together without the kids and it was the first time I'd been to London. We went

down on the train and stayed at the Green Park Hotel. I remember going to Petticoat Lane and walking around Piccadilly Circus on the Friday evening; I wanted to see the lights and the ladies of the night. On the Saturday we went to a show with Dora Bryan at the Prince of Wales Theatre. We went into this pub for a drink and a sandwich afterwards and she was behind us talking and she saw us, well we'd been sat near the front and I'd laughed so much that when George said something I nearly wet myself. She heard my laugh and came over and said, "You were on the second row, I'd recognise that laugh anywhere." She shoved my husband along the bench and sat talking to us. She was lovely, ordinary, like us.'

Rita's occasional winning trips to bingo gave the family their first holidays abroad.

'We had this thing come through the door – Halcyon Holidays – five days in Majorca at *El Arenal*. It was like the Blackpool of Majorca. And we went, the five of us, three boys plus me and him. It cost us and took us longer to get from here to Luton and stay overnight at Swiss Cottage in London. It was sixty pounds which was a lot of money.

Rita and George Whittle with their children and family friend Susan

'I remember once I went to the Mecca and won two-hundred pounds, which was a fortune. It was about 1972. We booked a holiday and went to Benidorm – with spending money. Train first, staying overnight in London and we got change out of two-hundred pounds. We went on a day trip while we were there and someone shouted, "Mrs

Whittle, I did your windows before we came away." My two eldest lads went out horse riding and they were gone ages and when they came back they'd been to a wedding up in the mountains and been given presents by all the locals.'

Throughout the years George was at sea, family holidays were rare and for most of the time, Rita would take the children to Humberston.

'My mum and dad had a caravan on the Fitties. Or we'd rent a bungalow for a fiver. My son Edward was saying he remembered going to Humberston and going out cockling and me cooking cockles on the Calor Gas stove. We had a good time.'

It would be the women in Mike Connor's community who organised street parties or the occasional trip to the boating lake.

'Even if the Methodist Church ran a do, it was the women who came round, it was the women that did it all the time. You see the men weren't involved in anything. All they did was come in, get drunk and go back to sea; they didn't even know what was going on.'

Missing his children while he was away at sea, Sally Wilbourne's husband Tom had sent a message on their behalf with completely unexpected consequences.

'Tom put a note in a bottle when he was fishing off the coast of Norway. And believe it or not we got an answer back. These people wrote and the friendship sort of went on and on and then they invited my girls over. It was a lot of money for us, so Tommy got a loan to pay for them to go over there and they went all the way there on their own. Flying from here to Amsterdam I think, and then they went from Amsterdam to somewhere else, and then they had to go on to a boat for the rest of the way into Norway. The friendship continued and the family used to write to us and everything. I've still got the letters and photographs.'

Another spur of the moment decision found Emma Brennan packing to take her children on an unexpected week's holiday.

'He landed in Whitby and he rung home and he said what a lovely place it was. He booked into a place called the Jolly Roger for a holiday for me and me two kids and he said he would be there waiting for me when he came home from sea. So we went for a week.'

The week was a rarity as Emma remembers; more often the family would take day trips out.

> 'Usually we'd go to Skegness for the day, just hop on a bus. We couldn't afford a car in them days. I used to take the kids on the ferry that used to run around Spurn. It was half a crown and you used to go down to the Royal Dock, get on the ferry and there used to be a man there playing an accordion, all the latest songs. I used to take the kids on a Sunday afternoon, "C'mon," I'd say, "we're going on the ferry," and we'd go round Spurn and back again all for two shillings and sixpence, lovely.'

In the days before the war, Margaret Monger's grandmother's cottage at Covenham was an idyllic holiday destination for her and her sisters.

> 'We were lucky in as much as with my grandma having the cottage, we spent our holidays there up until the war, roaming the countryside. And I mean roaming. We used to ride on the haycarts; we'd go down when they were bringing the harvest in and ride out. In 1938, he took a month off and hired a taxi and took us down to Essex, where he came from, and toured all the places he'd been. He was born in Harwich, and he'd been in the poorhouse and then he was orphaned. And then when he first started work at thirteen and a half, he was apprentice to a butcher at Dunmow, Essex. And when he was seventeen and a half, they were looking for apprentices so they took him from the butcher and apprenticed him here and so he became a fisherman.'

The difficulties in planning the simplest trip were commonplace for fishing families. On one occasion Janet Cox was looking forward to a bank holiday day out.

> 'I wanted to enjoy it like everybody else but they were due for sailing and I rang up to find out if they were sailing that day and got the message that, "Yeah we're going this afternoon." So we just went for the morning at Donna Nook instead with the kids and then hurried back, but the sailing got cancelled. We had about two hours out with the kids and then they didn't sail anyway.'

Set alongside the many other hardships and sacrifices of the lives of fishing families, perhaps the frustrations of not being able to have a holiday weren't one of the greatest concerns. However, as Janet points out, taking time ashore for a holiday would inevitably be a costly undertaking.

'We never went on holiday when the kids were small. First you'd have the cost of the holiday, then they would have to have a trip or two off to allow the boat to go to sea for them to be at home to go on holiday. And you can't just have one trip off and expect someone to take your place, you need to give them a couple of trips really if they're doing you a favour, give them the chance to earn some money while they do it. So it would have cost the price of the holiday plus two trips, so two or three times more. We could never have afforded it even though earnings were good. You couldn't afford to miss it in case you missed the good trips then come back and not earn much. I went camping, things like that, with my sister. We did have one or two holidays but it wasn't like a major part of the calendar.'

For many women, social lives revolved around children, families, friends and neighbours. It was rare for fishermen's wives to go out whilst their husbands were at sea. Olga Drever was one who rarely ventured out socially.

'When they came back we used to go to the pub, The Royal Hotel, never the Railway – that had a reputation. I did go out when he was away, but it was frowned on. You had to behave yourself, otherwise someone'd say, especially if you were dressed nice.'

Cleethorpes Winter Gardens 1959

Ann Graves remembers a Wednesday night out at Cleethorpes Winter Gardens' infamous 'Bags Ball' with husband Graham.

'Donkey's years ago before we was married, we went out to the Winter Gardens and Graham got into a barney with some fella - it's a wonder he never got leathered sometimes when his mouth started, but those that knew him and liked him knew there was no malice in him. And a couple of these fellas had gone wading in. And I remember distinctly putting my drink down and going in to sort it out. At the end

I look around and said, "Where was you?" He said, "What did you need me for?" He'd gone back and sat back down and the girl I went with, she'd said to him, "Your Ann's in there." He said, "Oh she can take care of herself and them an' all." He'd started it and he was sat there laughing at the time. I mean there was no fisticuffs but there was plenty of chat. Men in them days – they didn't hit a woman.

'The fishermen I knew, ninety-nine percent of 'em were gentlemen. You could go out and there was the good girls and the naughty girls and they knew the difference. You could go out, do your dancing – The Ship discotheque was the place to be then. It was the first disco in the town and that was the place to be and you could dance all night. You could go out with two shillings in your purse and start off with a glass of Coca-Cola and you could be on Bacardi and Coke all night long. They'd ask what you were drinking and look after you. Then at the end of the evening, they'd ask was I going home or if I wanted supper? It was alright as long as I was home by midnight. So you'd come out of the Ship's disco with whichever fisherman it was you knew and if he was hungry, it'd be, "C'mon lets go to the Chinese." The first in the town was at the riverhead there and you'd go down Victoria street and you'd go to the Chinese and they'd feed ya. Good company. And they were so smart. The only time you saw a fisherman without a suit on was sometimes on a landing day. They'd have a black suit, white shirt, red tie; thought they was the bees knees, fisherman's jackets with pleats at the back and a tight belt. Yeah, they was always turned out.'

Ann's husband Graham (second left) with crew members

Pete Woods remembers dressing up in the cast-off fishermen's clothes of his friend's older brothers.

'We used to get the Brylcream in our hair 'cos all the fishermen used to

> have a big wave in their hair and that. We used to wear their suits and black suede shoes. In the summer it was black suede shoes, white socks, grey slacks, white shirt and white cardigan – that was our outfit. Only fishermen ever wore the suits we had, which had the pleats down the back. So you had all these mini-fishermen roaming around twelve and thirteen year old.'

While there was camaraderie between fishermen, as Rita Whittle remembers, it wasn't always the case between the wives. As there was at sea, a distinct hierarchy existed ashore.

> 'I knew some of them through going out, but we were the lower end because we weren't skipper's or mate's wives. I remember once, we hadn't been in this house long and I was still decorating. They came back from a trip and we went to the Wheatsheaf, it was our favourite place in those days – you were someone if you went out there. We came home in a taxi, and I remember one woman - I think she was a mate's wife and I said, "You're more than welcome. I've no wallpaper up in the hall. I'm up to me neck in it; I'm going to finish off when he goes back to sea. But it's clean." And she sat there and said, "Well I'm not coming in." It was like that, snobbery. I didn't think anyone was better than me. I'll speak to anybody and help anybody, so my words to this woman – I'd had a couple of drinks - were, "You might be up the top now, but it's a quick drop."'

Annie Bell remembers the differences between the fishermen: skippers, mates, hands, deckies, and the firemen and engineers below decks.

> 'Oil and water doesn't mix. Them at the top didn't mix much with them at the bottom. They'd speak, they'd meet in a pub and buy each other a drink, but you see, the deck crew always talked about how much fish they'd caught, how much ice they'd used. Then somebody would say, "Well if it wasn't for the bloody engineers, the ship wouldn't move." Oh dear me, you could sit in a pub and they'd be at one another's throats in about an hour, but it wasn't malicious.'

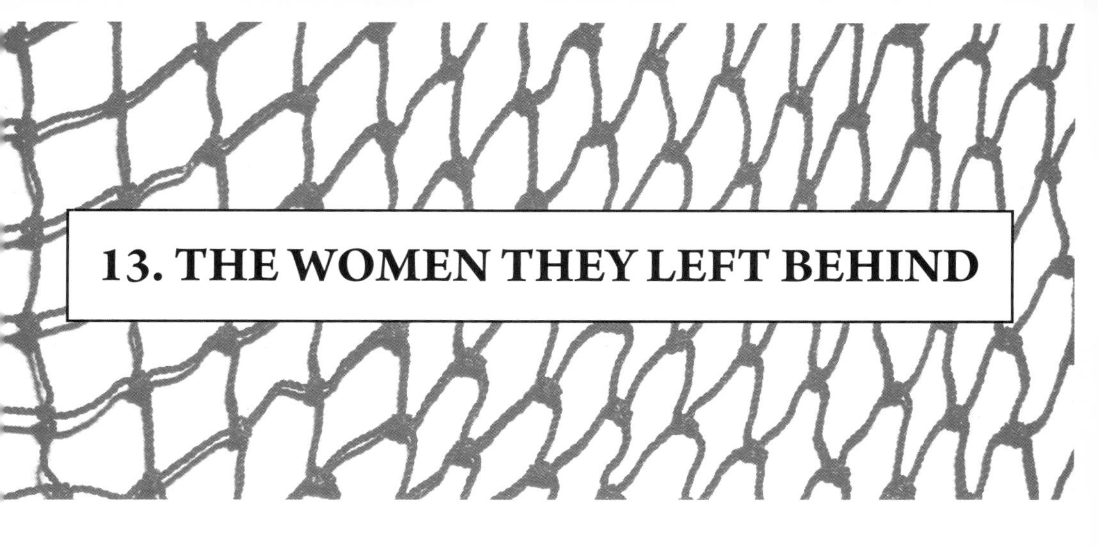

13. THE WOMEN THEY LEFT BEHIND

'... if the sea wants yer, it'll take yer.'

For those dependent on Grimsby's fishing industry, its eventual decline would come as a devastating blow. But for many families, the greatest losses happened while the industry was still very much working. Fishing was a dangerous occupation even with improved safety in later years. The threat of loved ones being lost was never far away. News of trouble at sea would send ripples of unease through the fishing community. Mike Connor remembers his mother's reaction to one such headline.

> 'She used to take us down Freeman Street, six of us in tow, and on the placard you'd read, "Grimsby Trawler Lost." Her face would turn pure white and she'd be shaking. She'd buy a newspaper and then she'd feel relief that it was some other poor bugger's husband they'd lost. I remember that happening on two or three occasions.'

Women were constantly reminded of the dangers their husbands and family members faced while at sea. They often had to endure the uncertainty of their men returning home when trawlers ran into trouble or bad weather. Olga Drever recalls her husband Steve's ship, the *Ross Puma,* running aground on the Little Rackwick shoals in 1968.

> 'It was the only time I ever got frightened. Steve's dad was an Orkney man and he passed away one trip when Steve was at sea. So when Steve's ship

docked, his mum asked would he take his dad's ashes and scatter them in the sea at the Pentland Firth, near the Old Man of Hoy. He scattered them on the first of April. Then a year later to the day, the phone went at six o'clock in the morning and it was the ship's runner, and he told me Steve's ship had gone aground. He wanted me to hear from him before I put the radio on. She'd gone on the rocks in bad weather by the Old Man of Hoy. The Long Hope Lifeboat came out and took the crew off one by one. When Steve was being taken off, he felt himself being pulled down into the water, then all of a sudden he felt himself being pushed up. He's not a superstitious sort of bloke, but he said he reckoned it was his dad pushing him up.'

The crew of the *Ross Puma* survived. Steve and his skipper stayed on Orkney to deal with the insurance claim. Staying at the Long Hope Hotel, they got to know the lifeboat crew. A year later the same crew were called to rescue the crew of a stricken tanker.

'Steve was on another ship in his cabin and it came on the news that the Long Hope lifeboat that had rescued them had gone over. All the crew were lost. He said he sat and sobbed. They're all relatives on the lifeboats, uncles, brothers – it's a family thing. He said they were such brave guys. They'd gone out to a tanker that was in distress and the lifeboat took a wave broadside and turned over. He never forgot about it.'

Tom Wilbourne (centre)

Working so closely together, many of the men formed close relationships and they took the losses hard. Mary-Rose Jessop's father was skipper of *The Hasset* in 1953. He lost two members of his crew when his ship went down.

'That day me dad come home, you could have cut the atmosphere with a knife. You don't realise the heartbreak they've all gone through.'

Allison Josefsen recalls how her friend tragically lost her husband and was lucky not to have suffered the same fate.

> 'They went to Tiburon, where he was from, to see his family. She went over on his fishing boat with him but he sailed and she came back separately on one of the butter boats. His boat went under and I think all they found was the lifebelt. To this day they've never found it. No bodies were ever found. I mean, if she hadn't stayed there a couple more days she wouldn't be here today. What do they say? God moves in mysterious ways and if the sea wants yer, it'll take yer.'

Some fishermen survived against the odds. Mike Connor's uncle Doug was presumed dead and gave the family quite a fright.

> 'We thought he'd got lost and all me aunties was there and me mother and me granny. And he walks in the back door. All the women screamed and me granny fainted. A wave had washed the bridge away and he clung on to this rail as he went overboard – this big strong Geordie – and all the women took me down to see and he still had his finger marks on this rail, they was there.'

For every one that had a lucky escape there were many more men that were lost, leaving behind family and friends. The after-effects of such an incident were not always evident until many years later. This is certainly the case for Maureen Harvey who has inherited her mother's deep-rooted fears of the sea.

> 'Me mum lost her first husband at Iceland in 1934, the whole ship went down. She frightened us. If we ever went near water she was absolutely petrified. None of us ever learned how to swim. She wouldn't take us. She was too frightened of it. We used to go down and meet me dad. She was always, "Come away, come away." She wouldn't let us near it. My husband can't believe I'm so frightened of water when my father was a fisherman.'

Ann Graves is one of many women for whom every detail of the loss of her husband resonates more than 30 years later.

> 'It was a Thursday, five-thirty/six o'clock on a beautiful sunny August morning and off Graham goes. I saw him off to the gate, he got in the taxi and then off he went. I watched while it went round the corner but he never turned round. That night at ten o'clock I was watching *My Wife Next Door* starring John Alderton and Hannah Gordon on the TV. The next morning before lunch, they came to tell me they'd found him at

eight o'clock that morning. When they used to go to sea, they'd have their kit bag in one hand and a crate of beer was in the other. And if he had a bob or two left, he always took what they called a crate, you got twenty-four cans, but they were smaller cans – *Worthington E* in a blue can. They'd gone into Scrabster and all gone ashore to the pub. As I say, Graham being unsociable, when they said they were going back to the ship for a party, he said, "Oh I'll get there when I get there, leave me on my own." And they did.

'I was told over the years that one or two of them felt guilty, but there was nothing for them to feel guilty about. I knew him and if he wasn't going, he wasn't going. At the time I thought, *why did they leave him?* D'you know what I mean? But nothing on earth would have made him go if he didn't want to. Nobody'd seen him since ten o'clock the night before when I was laid on the sofa watching… And in the morning they got ready to go to Iceland and they couldn't find him, so they searched the ship and he wasn't there. He was in the dock at the side of the ship. What the police put together was that, as he'd staggered back, he fell off the ladders going on ship. I've never been to Scrabster but apparently the dock's got a curve and the ships couldn't get as near. So that's how they found him. But we was lucky to get him back, that's how we looked at it. We buried him at Scartho. Oh dear, what a waste.

'I remember the day they came to tell me like it was yesterday. Mr Guilding, the chap that worked for Northern Trawlers, it was his job to come and give the news and he came with Mr Worton the Port Missioner at the time. It was a bright, sunny, warm August morning, and my little girl she was in the pram in the garden, washing just gone on the line, little boy playing in the garden, neighbours children… and just half an hour before I'd got the letter from the council to say that we'd got a house exchange and we was going into town. There was a knock on the door and I went and there was these two fellas stood there you see. Now in them days your insurance men came in twos when they was trying to sell you something. "Mrs Woods?" I said, "I don't want nothing. Whatever you've got I don't want it. I'm not buying nothing." And with that, one put his foot in the door you see, and I got a little annoyed. "Ay watch what you're doing, on yer way. I don't want anything." He said, "No, you don't know who we are Mrs Woods. Can we come in? We're from Northern Trawlers."

'Half a dozen houses from us lived another fisherman and his wife and he was just coming from the paper shop as he saw these getting out the car. Mr Guilding knew him and he said, "Oh Trevor will you just wait and come..." Trevor was like, "No, no I won't," and he couldn't get away fast enough. "I'll send my missus." He knew what they'd come for. Apparently he'd gone running in and said to his wife, "Get round to Ann's and I'll run round and get Shirley," - she's my cousin who was their friend.

'The next thing I remember is that the house seemed to be full of people and I was laid on the sofa being sick in a bowl and the Port Missioner was holding my head. Mr Guilding had to go get my mother and she worked down at the clothing shop. The next thing I remember was the funeral at the Fisherman's Chapel in Duncombe Street.'

As a young wife and mother, Ann struggled to deal with Graham's death.

'They used to shell out valium like sweets at the doctors. I must have had some sense, because I was frightened of getting reliant on them. But for nearly ten years, I always had some in the house. For the first two or three months or maybe six, I can't remember much at all and that's when I think, *thank God for me mother* and then me dad when he came home from the hospital cause I'd have never have made it.

'I used to go up to the cemetery every day, until the doctor told my mum she'd got to keep me away. You can't afford to do that when you've got two babies and nobody else to look after 'em, but at the time you don't think. Well you're not thinking are you? You just don't know.

'One night when the bairns were in bed, I was sat there and the night was wearing on and on and I thought, *I can't take this anymore. I can't do this anymore. I just want to go.* We all climbed in bed together, snuggled down and went to sleep. I dreamed I was at the gates of heaven, these pearly gates, and I've got Kelly in one hand and I'm holding Zane's hand in the other. It opens and Graham is stood there and he took the babies off me and he wouldn't let me in. And he said, "No you go back and do it on your own." I woke up and in all the years I was by myself, in all the years after that, it never entered my head again because I knew he would never ever forgive me. And I don't care what anybody tries to tell me – I saw him, and he was mad with me. I won't say I didn't get that far down again,

> but letting go never ever entered my head again.'

Although Ann struggled to cope she was afraid to ask for help from anyone other than her immediate family.

> 'You didn't tell anyone you needed help in those days, because the first thing they did was take your children off you. The first thing that Mr Worton the Port Missioner said, after things were over and had started to settle a little bit, "I must say this Ann because it's my job and I've got to… We can take your children and put them in the Seaman's and Sailors Home in Hull." *Woah, they're not having my kids!* Do you know what I mean? Because I would have never have got through it without them. But I know I was offered the choice. I think maybe it was *that* that made me not ask for any help from anybody. My mam gave me the help and my dad for the short time he was here later. You didn't ask for help because if you couldn't manage they would come and take 'em.
>
> 'I remember Kelly was about two – she was about eighteen months when her dad went – and I was at my mum's house in the front room. Me mum was in the kitchen and we both thought Kelly was with each other and she was in my mum's back room. And my mum, in her drawer in the side board, had her medication and Kelly had these tablets in her hand and she was sucking them. Well, we got it out of her and got a taxi straight away, straight up to the hospital. It was the old hospital then. They pumped her out, poor little thing. Luckily she hadn't taken anything she'd just started to suck one. They pumped her out and she had to stay in overnight. I went to get her the next morning with my mum and they wouldn't let her come out and we had to see the paediatrician. She was concerned about this rash that Kelly had at the time, well kids get rashes don't they? She said, "Well I'm going to let you go home, but I want to keep an eye on it," which was fair enough. A couple of days later there's a knock on my front door and who's stood there but this little woman in a uniform. Now she used to be what we called our dick nurse and she was then a district nurse. "Hello Ann." And she's come in the door and I says, "Ay what do you want?" She said I've come to keep an eye on yer. Ooh me language and I told her in no uncertain terms to get on 'er bike. She said, "We've got to keep a check on all these things, if you're not looking after 'em properly."

Graham, Ann, Kelly and Zane

> '"Where was you when me husband died?' I said. "No help at all. Go away. I've got all the help I want." She said she'd come back. I said, "You can do as you like but you're not coming in this house." And I really sent her off with a flea in her ear and luckily I never heard anything else.'

With the support of family, friends and the Fishermen's Mission, Ann fought back and eventually re-married. Her memories of Graham are never far away. She remembers an encounter with one of Graham's former crew mates soon after the accident.

> 'We were walking down Freeman Street, Kelly in her pushchair and Zane with me mum, and there's this young lad, Graham's mate from his ship, coming up and he stopped dead and went as white as a ghost. He couldn't get away quick enough and he went in Woolworths. They couldn't face anybody. Whether it made a difference in me, it doesn't matter. Over the years, even before I lost my second husband if I see anybody and I know they've had a bereavement I go out of my way to stop and speak and I mention them who's gone. I always ask, "Are you alright talking about them?" I can't remember anybody over the years saying, "No I don't talk." You want to talk about them, because while you talk about them, they're not gone.'

In spite of the frequent losses at sea, it was a death at home which finally made Marjorie Louis's husband, George, give up fishing.

> 'He'd always been at sea. He was on the oil rigs about two year then he came home and he used to do two weeks on and a week off. Then we lost my eldest son, Paul. He was fourteen. I don't know where it come from, but polystyrene used to wash up, and him and his mate decided to make a raft and it took 'em out. Well his mate could swim and swam back and said to Paul, "Stay on the raft. I'll go and get help." We don't know to this day whether he tried to swim or something got him under, but he was washed up at four o'clock the next day, and that was 25 June 1970. Paul would have gone to sea. He said the first trip he did he was going to buy me a radiogram. He was adamant he was going to be a fisherman. After Paul died, George said, "I've left you all these years, landed you with a house full of kids, and I'm never ever going away to leave you again." And he never went away from that day until I lost him.'

Through generations of fishing in Grimsby, The Fishermen's Mission has offered help and support to many families during the most difficult times. Dawn Wraith's husband Andy died of cancer. Recently she benefited from their practical financial support.

> 'I didn't know about getting fishermen's money for Jay my grandson until four of five years ago, and me daughter-in-law, a neighbour of hers, her

> husband was a skipper... and she told me you could get some money. I applied to Mr Worton. When Andy died I couldn't get a penny, and they said it was an act of God. I was so bitter about that. If Andy had died at sea of an injury I'd have got the money, but because he died of what they call an act of God, I never got money. It's so cruel. But I get forty eight pounds a month from the mission for Jay. I had to get in touch with Mr Dolby first and he came to see me and he says to me, "Have you got any bills you owe?" I said I might have a catalogue. Do you know, they paid the catalogue off. I think it was about three-hundred pounds. I couldn't believe it. I just cried when he went, it was such a relief to me. In August, they get sixty-pounds for a clothing grant from The Fishermen's Mission, from the one at Family and Sailors Society at Hull, it's done through Mr Dolby. I rung him not long ago because my washer played up and me daughter-in-law said I should ring him. So anyhow, I thought, *I won't ring him I'll write a letter*. He came to see me and I had a washer in two weeks, he said, "You've only got to ask."'

Graham Dolby is the recently retired Port Missioner for Grimsby. He follows in the footsteps of countless men and women who served their local fishing communities.

> 'If there was a loss, if a ship had gone down, maybe all hands, or even if it was just one man overboard who was lost, it was the mission very often who were notified first and so it was the port missioner who was expected to go round and break the news. When the mission man was seen going down the street everybody almost stopped to see which house he was going to... it's unfortunate that you got a little bit of a reputation by being there to help, and you'd go in and support, not just a wife but sometimes a mother with quite a number of children. We just had to help them. Many families have been helped by the mission so I think they tend to lean on the mission man, particularly in times of difficulty. I remember one man saying to me, "My first recollection of a mission man was as he stepped over me on the doorstep, he came to tell mam that dad wasn't coming back." That's how life was, so I think you became part of their families to a large extent. You're greeted as a member of the family. You go in and you're made to feel very welcome. It's a privilege.'

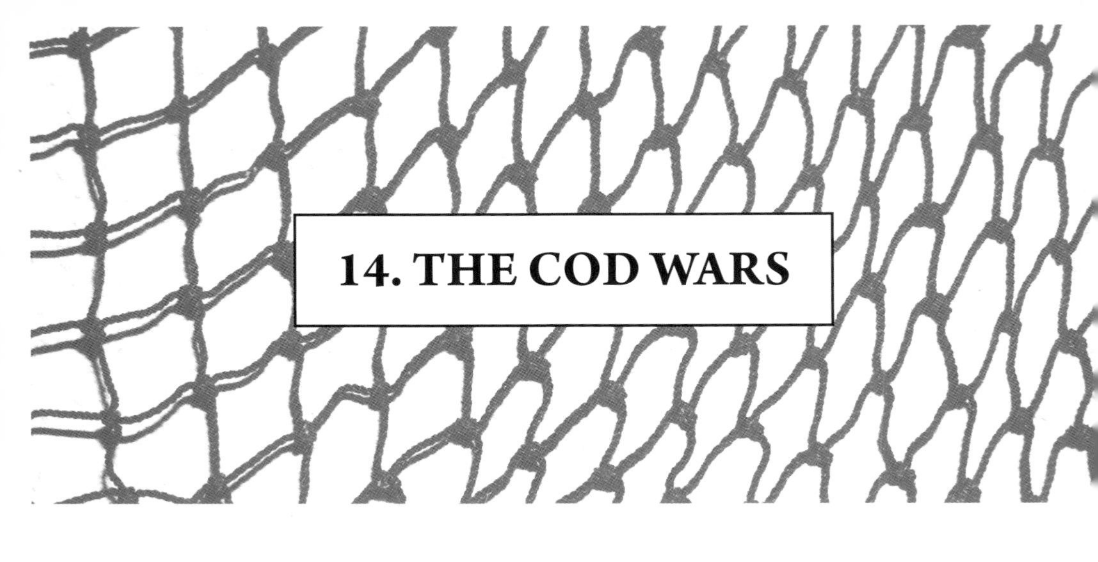

14. THE COD WARS

'... you're talking about war – it was war. I nearly 'ad me head took off by a shot.'

The roots of the conflict that became the cod wars between Britain and Iceland can be traced to the earliest part of the 20th century. On 23 June 1901, Denmark signed a Treaty with Britain establishing a three mile territorial limit around Iceland, then a Danish dependency, and the Faroe Islands. Icelanders referred to the Treaty as 'the bacon and butter agreement' believing the Danes had signed in order to access British markets.

With an economy dependant on the fishing industry, Iceland considered the preservation of fish stocks and prevention of over-fishing of paramount national importance, taking up the matter in the *International Council for the Exploration of the Sea* in 1937. In August 1946, the Council passed a Resolution recommending the closure of one of the most important fishing grounds in the world for 10 years - *Faxa Bay,* situated off Iceland's western coast.

In 1950 the Icelandic Government issued *Regulations Concerning the Conservation of Fishing Banks off the North Coast of Iceland*. This prohibited trawling and seine-netting by all vessels, Icelandic and foreign, in bays off Iceland's north coast, as well as within a four mile limit from baselines drawn across the bays.

Britain, France, Belgium, and the Netherlands protested, believing Iceland was depriving them of their right to fish, and that she had no right to unilaterally extend fishing limits. However, there was no general rule of International Law prescribing the three mile limit and no rule prohibiting a state from extending its limits. British opposition was the most severe and on the 2 May 1952 the British Government sent a note to the Icelandic Government in protest, pointing out that:

> '...for over half a century British fishing vessels have fished in waters from which they are now excluded under the new regulations and for a large part of this period there was in force a treaty between the two countries regulating fishery limits.'

British trawler owners imposed a landing ban on Icelandic trawlers in British harbours, despite the fact that the new regulations applied to Icelandic as well as foreign vessels. The landing ban was lifted by an agreement between the two countries on the 15 November 1956.

Battle lines for the first cod war were effectively drawn when, in July 1956, Hermann Jonasson's government came to power in Iceland and issued a statement that included a clause on the extension of fishery limits:

> '...the government... is of the opinion that an increasing of the conservation areas around the country is now a pressing necessity for the security of employment of the nation and will therefore do its utmost to implement this policy'.

The First Cod War

On 1 September 1958, Iceland extended its fishing limits from four to 12 miles. *The Conference on the Law of the Sea* in April 1958 saw the participation of 86 states, most of whom supported the establishment of a six mile limit. The United States proposed six miles plus a further contiguous fishery zone of six miles. Britain reluctantly agreed to support the proposal, with certain conditions.

Prior to the conference, Grimsby skippers and mates had threatened that, should the conference result in deadlock, they would call for a ban on Icelandic landings and, if necessary, enforce the ban by refusing to sail. Fears for the future of the industry increased when it was announced on 4 June 1958 that the Faroe Islands were to extend fishery limits to 12 miles, effectively closing to British fishing from 1 September. Grimsby was one of the leading Faroe fishing ports.

Cyril Osborne MP for Louth, Chancellor of the Exchequer and Minister of Agriculture, Fisheries, and Food was told that a 12 mile limit imposed by Iceland would see the loss to Grimsby of 75% of the fish caught in Icelandic waters between January and May. The British Trawler Federation warned its members and the Government that:

> '...if we do get 12 miles, within a very few years... there will be no industry'.

However, the British Government could do little to stop Iceland extending her limits and the Icelandic Government made plain their intention to punish any vessel caught breaking the law. Talks were held in Grimsby in August 1958 to explain the Government's position: the Royal Navy would operate a modified version of the wartime convoy system to protect British trawlers.

The first incident to directly involve a Grimsby trawler occurred on 1 September 1958, when the Royal Navy prevented an attempt by Icelandic gunboats to arrest the Grimsby trawlers, *Coventry City* and *Vascama*. The Icelandic gunboat *Albert* sailed alongside *Coventry City* and when it was 50 yards away shouted a message across to warn the skipper he was fishing illegally three miles inside the new limit. *Coventry City's* skipper replied that he was fishing outside the four mile limit which he recognised as the official one. The frigate *Russell* positioned itself between the vessels causing *Albert* to sail off.

Grimsby Evening Telegraph

FINAL

'Good morning' says the captain of a British 'watchdog'—but he gets no reply

ICELANDIC GUNBOATS FOILED

Navy races in—stops attempts to arrest Grimsby trawlers

THE ROYAL NAVY TODAY FOILED ATTEMPTS BY ICELANDIC GUNBOATS TO ARREST TWO GRIMSBY TRAWLERS, THE COVENTRY CITY AND THE VASCAMA, ONLY A FEW HOURS AFTER THE DISPUTED 12-MILE LIMIT CAME INTO FORCE AT MIDNIGHT.

Skipper gives a tip-off

Heard broadcast

'Stop instantly'

Newlyweds killed in car crash

DEATH OF MR. I. M. CULE

WATCHES AS SHIPS FISH

UPROAR AT T.U.C. OVER UNION DELEGATE ISSUE

ANDERBY CREEK DROWNING

SCUNTHORPE BOY (2) FOUND SAFE AFTER BIG SEARCH

Dog disappeared

All-night hunt

Prince Bernhard in car crash

SOLDIER IN CYPRUS IS SHOT DEAD FROM BEHIND

New standard

H.M.S *Palliser* came to the aid of *Vascama* fishing five and a half miles off Horn, Iceland's most northerly point. The Icelandic gunboat *Aegir* was seen closing in and a signal for the trawler to stop was sent. *Palliser* came up astern, positioning itself between the vessels until the trawler finished hauling.

A more serious incident occurred the following day when the Icelandic gunboats, *Thor* and *Marie Julia* intercepted the Grimsby trawler *Northern Foam* seven miles off shore. She was boarded and her skipper ordered aboard one of the Icelandic vessels. He refused and was ordered by British frigate H.M.S *Eastbourne,* who had been informed of the events by *Foam's* wireless operator, to immobilise his ship and ignore the Icelanders' requests. As *Eastbourne* approached more Icelanders boarded, took the trawler by force and began to take her away at full speed. *Eastbourne* again ordered *Foam's* skipper to immobilise and shortly after the trawler stopped. *Eastbourne* sent aboard 14 men who regained control.

TRELLIS LATHS

THE GRIMSBY TIMBER Co. Ltd

ALEXANDRA ROAD, GRIMSBY.

WEATHER

LIGHTING-UP

TODAY'S TIDES

Grimsby Evening Telegraph

FINAL

GRIMSBY CO-OP

HOOVER

H.M.S. Eastbourne to the rescue after gunboats board the Northern Foam

NAVY 'RECAPTURES' SHIP

GRIMSBY VESSEL IN LIMITS DRAMA

'Repel Boarders'—and Grimsby men resist

UNDER cover of thick fog at 8 o'clock this morning two Icelandic gunboats boarded and seized by force the Grimsby trawler Northern Foam. But their attempt to take the vessel into port was foiled by the British frigate Eastbourne which, after a dramatic dash, sent over her own naval boarding party and regained control of the trawler.

Radio operator locks himself in cabin

During the boarding — in the fishing "haven" north of the Papey Islands, about eight miles off the south-east coast of Iceland — the Northern Foam's wireless operator locked himself in his radio room to maintain contact with the Royal Navy fishery protection ships nearby.

CHILDREN KILLED AS AIRLINER PLUNGES

On 22 September the *Marie Julia* made a further attempt to board a Grimsby trawler, the *Lincoln City*. The *Lincoln City's* crew lined up at the railings with axes and lumps of coal, deterring the Icelanders. However, it was not always Icelanders who initiated encounters. On 10 September the 486 ton Grimsby trawler *King Sol* rammed the Icelandic gunboat *Odinn*. News of the ramming came through from *King Sol's* skipper, who reported that the *Odinn* tried to pull alongside him so, he:

> '...went astern into him, and made a right nice mark on his bow.'

An agreement to end the conflict came on 11 March 1961 when Britain sent a note to the Icelandic Government stating that it no longer objected to 12 mile fishery zone around Iceland. It was negotiated that for three years from March 1961, Iceland would not object to British vessels fishing during certain months of the year in specified areas between six and 12 miles from shore. It was also agreed that during the period of adjustment, UK vessels would not fish inside the 12 mile zone in seven specified areas. The Government had reached an agreement which, in the short term, would be less harsh on Britain's distant-water fleet.

In reaction to the agreement, Grimsby trawler skippers, mates and engineers threatened strike action if Icelandic trawlers landed or attempted to land fish at the port. A joint meeting of the Grimsby Trawler Officers Guild and the Grimsby Steam and Diesel Fishing Vessels Engineers and Firemen's Union declared that:

> '... in view of the Icelandic Parliament having accepted the proposed terms of the existing Icelandic dispute, if any Icelandic trawler lands, or attempts to land, in the Port of Grimsby, then the skippers, mates, and engineers will be withdrawn from all Grimsby trawlers.'

Members of both organisations felt strongly that Grimsby would be hardest hit as a result of the agreement, since 90% of its distant-water trawlers fished in the area off the north-west coast of Iceland, which the agreement closed to British trawlers.

The unions considered the areas British trawlers were permitted to fish to be unsubstantial fishing grounds. The agreement also established a precedent for other countries to extend their own limits to 12 miles, excluding British trawlers. On 4 April, unions were advised that an Icelandic trawler was approaching, and true to their word, trawler officers and engineers went on strike. The unions released a statement:

> '...we hope that the British housewife will realise that every bit of frozen fish she buys could be a nail in the coffin of British trawler men.'

Several unsuccessful attempts were made by trawlers to sail in an effort to beat the strike. On 5 and 6 April, the *Boston Vanguard* tried to leave port. On its second attempt, a crowd of fishermen, dockers and lumpers gathered at the quay and cries of 'traitor' could be heard. Crew members leapt ashore as the trawler pulled away from the quay, fearing the consequences of breaking the strike. The skipper returned to port.

The dispute ended on 13 May when the Grimsby Trawler Officers Guild withdrew its strike notice and the first trawler to leave the port in 39 days prepared to sail. Now, only the engineers were still officially on strike. The deckhands had also returned to work on the 13 May. On 17 May the engineers returned to work and the strike was finally over after 42 days.

On 11 March 1964, the three year period of adjustment ended. Britain had been preparing for this, and at her request, a European Fisheries Conference was held in London from December 1963 until March 1964. The Conference agreed to a document, *The European Fisheries Convention*, which stated that the governments of Austria, Belgium, Denmark, France, the Federal Republic of Germany, Ireland, Italy, Luxemburg, the Netherlands, Portugal, Spain, Sweden, and the UK, agreed to establish a 12 mile limit with a concession for each of them to fish up to six miles of each others shores for 10 years. In establishing her own 12 mile limit, Britain effectively excluded herself from any concessions inside Iceland's own limit.

On 13 June 1971, Iceland elected Olafur Johanneson as its new Prime Minister.

The first item on the new government's policy statement was concerned with the extension of fishery limits, proposing:

> '...that the fisheries agreement within Britain and the federal Republic of Germany be abrogated and a decision made on the extension of the fishery limit to fifty miles from baselines, and that this extension be implemented no later than 1 September 1972.'

The Icelandic government deemed a further extension of the fishery limits essential:

> '...to safeguard the vital interests of the Icelandic people'.

Britain took the view that the 1961 agreement was still in force and maintained Iceland had no right to further extend its limits. Unsuccessful meetings were held in an attempt to resolve the position. The International Court of Justice had no means of enforcing a ruling, and so when Iceland extended its limits to 50 miles, despite the courts finding in favour of Britain, they could only observe the action. Once again, vessels from all states fishing in Icelandic waters respected the new limits except Britain and Germany, whose trawlers continued to fish up to 12 miles off the Icelandic coast.

The Second Cod War

In September 1972 Iceland extended its fishing limits from 12 to 50 miles.

By the time of the second cod war, Icelandic coastguard crews had been trained in using the trawler wire cutter. Every coastguard ship was equipped. If trawlers refused to leave the area on request, the coastguard would sail across the vessel's stern with trawler wire cutters lowered into the sea and drawn behind it, thus cutting the wires of the offending trawler. Irate British crews tried to deter Icelandic coastguard vessels, either by ramming or using a pair of trawlers to operate a single trawl.

British skippers demanded that further protection of their vessels be provided, and in turn trawler owners demanded protection from the British Government. The Government rented four tug-boats, the *Englishman, Irishman, Lloydsman,* and *Statesman,* and sent them to Icelandic waters to protect trawlers. On 17 May 1973 British skippers informed the British Government they would not continue to fish unless the Royal Navy deployed. The British Government yielded to pressure groups from Grimsby and Hull and sent Royal Navy frigates into Icelandic waters.

Life was tough enough for fishermen's wives. For Rose Blake whose husband, Harry, was mate on a Grimsby trawler, the television news reports brought home the added danger fishermen faced.

> 'What was frightening when the cod war was on, was not hearing from him or anything. His mother kept saying, "Have you heard from Harry?" I said, "No. Not yet." We was all worried. Then we got a telegram saying he was safe and not to worry. He never told me about accidents at sea. He did tell other people. He knew that it'd upset me.'

Pete Hickson and Derek Brown fished out of Grimsby during the cod wars. Pete remembers an overflight by an RAF Nimrod carrying a government minister.

> 'I mean you're talking about war – it was war. I nearly 'ad me head took off by a shot. Some people say they did a good job at the time but... there was a lot of this chopping of waters and ramming and all that lot. It all went on. We won - the Royal Navy cleared the Icelandic Coastguard off the ocean. But then the British government paid the Icelandic Coast Guard to go to Denmark to have their bloody ships repaired! We paid for the damage that the Navy had done to their ships. Yeah we won the battle but lost the war.'

The conflict ended with another piecemeal agreement. British fleets would be permitted to fish in certain areas within the 50 mile limit. Britain also agreed to a 130,000 ton limit on the number of fish that could be caught by British trawlers. The agreement was valid for two years. When it expired on 13 November 1975 the third cod war began almost immediately.

The Third Cod War

In July 1975, the Icelandic Government issued regulations extending its fisheries limits to 200 nautical miles to take effect from 15 October 1975. Once again, British and German fishermen were the only ones who did not respect the new limit. British fishermen re-visited their strategies. The British ambassador in

Reykjavik made an announcement at the ministry for foreign affairs in Reykjavik on 25 November:

> 'Her Majesty's Government have decided to provide naval protection to enable British trawlers to continue fishing off Iceland in the face of efforts by Icelandic coastguard vessels to stop them. H.M.C *Leopard* which is already on its way to the area, will reach the fishing grounds later today...'

The third was the most violent of the conflicts. Royal Navy vessels rammed Icelandic coastguard ships 17 times between December 1975 and February 1976. Trawlerman Derek Brown recalls the degree to which communication between the Royal Navy and fishing vessels was fundamental to ensure fishing could be carried out.

> 'There were one incident where they (naval escorts) were told to lay off and so they trailed the Icelandic gun boats, each one followed one and they would come on and give a report at say, half past the hour. And they'd say, "This is HMS *Broadsword* and we're trailing the *Aegir.*" And they'd give you a location so you knew where the gun boats were and you could grab a bit of fishing time before they got there to chop your gear.
>
> 'Well this mate of mine, Roy, was in a ship called the *Vivaria* which was one of the fastest in the dock. We was down on the whaleback edge and a gun boat comes you see, this *Aegir.* So Roy says, "I'll chase him off." So he's chasing, and the guy's running and he gets about twenty mile away, then *Aegir* turns and starts to chase the *Vivaria*. So Roy's steaming back and he's calling, "*HMS Broadsword, HMS Broadsword* this is *Vivaria, Vivaria.*"
> "*Vivaria* this is *Broadsword* go ahead with your message, skipper."
> "The *Aegir's* chasing and gaining on me all the time!"
> "*Aegir's* chasing and gaining. Okay skipper message received. Out."
> So then a bit later, "*HMS Broadsword, HMS Broadsword* this is *Vivaria.*'
> "*Vivaria* this is *Broadsword* go ahead with your message skipper."
> "I tell you this *Aegir* is gaining on me all the time, it's gonna run right into me!"
> "Er yes, skipper, message received. Out."
> So when Roy comes on again, and he's panicky by now 'cos *Aegir's* very close, he says, "*Broadsword, Broadsword* this is the *Vivaria*. The *Aegir's* close, if he gets much closer he'll disappear right up my arse!"

The trawler *Vivaria*

Broadsword came back, "*Vivaria* this is *Broadsword,* Captain speaking. Skipper, if rape is inevitable, enjoy it."
And Roy went, "Did you hear that?!""

On 8 January 1976 the Icelandic cabinet passed a resolution on measures to be taken in response to aggression in Icelandic waters, concluding that:

'The Icelandic Government considers it inevitable that a continuation of deliberate ramming by British warships on Icelandic coastguard vessels will lead to severing of diplomatic relations with Great Britain.'

A request was made to the Secretary General of NATO to visit Iceland to discuss the issue. He arrived in Iceland on 14 January and subsequently had discussions in London; neither yielded positive results. On the 19 January the Icelandic Government resolved that:

> 'Should British warships and Nimrod aircraft still be operating within the Icelandic 200 mile fisheries limits by 12 o'clock midnight GMT on 24 January 1976, the Government of Iceland will consider diplomatic relations between Iceland and Great Britain to be severed...'

The British Government announced that they would withdraw warships and the Icelandic Prime Minister was invited to London for talks with Harold Wilson. These were unsuccessful and once again, the Royal Navy were deployed in Icelandic waters.

Several diplomatic attempts were made to resolve the dispute. The matter was taken up in the U. N. Security Council and the NATO Council but without success. The American Government pushed for a solution, mainly as a result of Iceland threatening to close the NATO base at Keflavik. Britain was coming under increasing international pressure.

There is a strong sense of irony that the task of ending the conflict fell to Foreign Secretary and Grimsby MP Anthony Crosland. Crosland's arrival at the Foreign

Office coincided with the frequent clashes between British trawlers and Icelandic gunboats, and despite pressure from his own constituency, he requested a meeting with Icelandic ministers. The meeting at the Icelandic Embassy in Oslo concluded that both sides would maximise attempts to reach an agreement at a further meeting to be held a week later. On 1 June an agreement was reached, and diplomatic relations between Iceland and Britain resumed. The agreement, approved on 11 November 1976, was that Britain was to limit its fishing effort in Icelandic waters, with only 24 trawlers from a list of 93 allowed to fish at any one time, in some places as close to 20 miles to the shore. In addition, four conservation areas were completely closed and the amount of cod Britain could catch was limited to 50,000 tons a year.

The duration of the agreement was six months, and after it expired on 1 December 1976 it was not renewed. Crosland's position was damaged; there were fears that he may not have been re-elected. However, Anthony Crosland died at his home in Adderbury in January 1977. When Austin Mitchell was elected as Grimsby's MP in April of that year, the fleet was tied down, with vessels moored on Grimsby Docks' North Wall. It would be Mitchell's task to begin the fight for compensation.

The cod wars had a profound effect on the fishing families of Grimsby and justifiable bitterness at the outcome was compounded by what followed. Margret Robinson is one of many still angry at Anthony Crosland's involvement.

> 'He didn't seem to do anything about it. Crosland didn't fight it, he was a yes man, he signed the rights away. His wife had the audacity to sprinkle his ashes on the water off the North Wall, when he'd took their livelihood.'

Mary-Rose Jessop is another who feels the British Government gave in too easily.

> 'Crosland let the Icelanders walk all over us. I don't know why. I mean John, my first husband, was out there when the first fish war was going on. You know the gun boats were guarding the ships, and I used to be worried sick. I mean you get one of them gun boats - we had a seine netter - they start circling... and they're allowed to board ya – they'd have us, and it's frightening, really frightening. But I think Crosland sold us all down the line, it was as simple as that.'

15. THE WRITING ON THE WALL

'... the expenses were more than the fish they'd got so there'd be nothing left to share.'

Iceland's final extension of fishing limits was a crucial blow to Grimsby, but the move to protect her fishing industry was inevitable. Catching fish to ship to the UK was the only way she could support her population.

Equally significant in the UK industry's decline was the *Common Fisheries Policy* the Heath Government signed in 1972, which gave European partners access to British waters. Hindsight makes the presumption that fishing in Icelandic waters would continue indefinitely appear naive. When the agreement to end the third cod war was signed in 1976, Britain was unable to compensate for distant water losses by developing fishing in her own waters.

The industry ran down gradually as some men moved to middle and near-water vessels. A drastic decline in the numbers of Grimsby's distant-water vessels meant that only six of British United Trawlers' distant-water fleet remained. When these moved to Hull, Grimsby was left as a middle and near-water port. By 1977, there were only around 100 fishing vessels left in Grimsby. Now there are around 20, many of these landing their catch in Scotland, Belgium or Holland with the great majority of fish now sold on Grimsby's fish market sent from Iceland and the Faroe Islands.

For some the writing had been on the wall as far back as the late 1960s, when advertisements began to appear in local newspapers tempting British fishermen to work abroad. One evening while her husband was at sea, Olga Drever had been reading the *Grimsby Evening Telegraph* and noticed an advert placed by Irvine and Johnson, a Glasgow-based company, looking for skippers and mates to work in South Africa.

> 'Steve called them when he came in. He got the job and was on the crew that took the *Boston Weelsby* out to South Africa. He stayed to set up and we followed about six months later. We lived in Capetown and Steve worked on the freezer trawlers. Sometimes they were away for six weeks sometimes longer, but the difference in going to sea there and going here, well there was the weather for a start, which was great. Steve didn't think twice about going. I was homesick when we first went. My son was fourteen when he went to school there. He didn't like it, but it made him.'

Steve and Olga's travels didn't end there; a spell on Tristan De Cuhna, an isolated volcanic island in the South Atlantic, saw Steve managing a crayfish factory.

> 'We had to take stores with us. There were two hundred and forty-eight people on the island and we had a lovely little house looking out over the sea. Steve managed the factory and occasionally went for a day out with the fishermen from the island, only small boats. And believe it or not, he used to be seasick.

The trawler *Boston Weelsby*

> 'When we came home to South Africa, the firms were picking white engineers to employ black workers as cheap labour. We met some fantastic guys there. There was a time he'd come off the docks in Capetown, you

come through the gates and there's a pub called *The Queens*, a seamen's pub and he had one of the other engineers or one of the mates with him. And he went in the pub and they wouldn't serve the black blokes. Serve Steve, but not them. And he said, "I've been at sea six weeks alongside these chaps. Put that pint back. If they can't have a drink, I can't have a drink."

'We lived there for twenty years. Then, in 1990, we came back. And the very last ship we saw when we went from Cape Town to Durban to come home as we left the harbour was the *Boston Weelsby*. People used to say we were mad for coming back to Grimsby, but you get homesick. And I had children here too. Steve still had another five years of work left so he decided to go on the oil rigs, well, on the standby ships as Chief Engineer, which he did until he stopped work. The town had changed a helluva lot, but y'know, you fall into it again.'

Doreen Tyson's brother was another who looked for an opportunity abroad, making the trip to Australia in the mid-1970s.

'It was about 1976. He went on a trawler. I think it was almost a full Grimsby crew went over; they sailed from Hull and it was something to do with British United Trawlers. As I remember, British United Trawlers and the Australian government formed a company out there for them to fish and they were going to give it a year to see how it went. My brother came home on leave after a year and apparently they'd decided not to continue with this company, but he'd enjoyed the life out there so much that he got a job as a taxi driver, applied for a visa and paid his fare back to Australia.

'He kept fishing, but it wasn't the sort of fishing you did here... it wasn't for haddock, cod and things like that... it was big prawns, shell fishing, factory fishing and they used to go for three or four months at a time as far as the Persian Gulf or down to Antarctica, wherever they could get you know. He loved it, absolutely loved it. And he got his skipper's ticket over there in Australia. A lot of Hull and Grimsby fishermen went out there; there was a tight community of fishermen that's gradually dispersing now, but they used to congregate in the pubs when they were all in from sea.'

As one of the few women whose husband still sails from Grimsby, Janet Cox has seen the decline first hand.

'It didn't affect us too much at first - because it was the big boats that went at the start and the small boats were doing okay for a number of years. I think it first hit us when our kids were teenagers. From being comfortable and earning good – you know it was worth them going away for the reward they got back then. It would've affected us in the late 1970s. So I went out to work. They could go away and not earn anything. They'd do a trip and not catch much and the expenses were more than the fish they'd got so there'd be nothing left to share.

'He would retire if he could. I mean to be honest, if his brother decided to sell the boat and stop tomorrow that'd probably be it anyway. There wouldn't be any other boats down there to get another job. Be alright if we could manage. But you don't get a pension until you're sixty-five so you wouldn't have an income.

'A lot of the work now is guarding pipelines, not fishing. They just sail up and down and protect pipes on the sea bed, you know gas pipes things like that, if they're being laid or if they are exposed, to stop other boats trawling over them and damaging them. They fish in between, it varies. They just have to keep changing what they fish for all the time. It's like they've just been prawning – that was in the North Sea. Most of the fishing is in the North Sea. But they just have to change with whatever is profitable.

'There was a point quite a few years later where I thought he might be able to get on the standby boats where it's like a month away and then a month at home, steady money all the time. But by then they needed to have certificates to get them. Like if they used to be skippers or skippers' mates or whatever but he didn't have any certificates so he didn't get in there either. I don't think he really wanted to come out of the fishing industry anyway.

'We had some good times in the early years. There was that community feeling – always others around in the same situation. You weren't the odd one out you know. It was normal for them to be away and miss everything but you had each other. Obviously now I'm sort of the only one. I've found it harder as I've got older - when you're younger you've got all your children around and you fill your life up with other stuff. Now the kids have gone and I am on my own when he's away. You don't hang around together like you do when you've all got children. It's pretty tough really. People just think: *Oh you're used to it anyway because you've done it all your life,* but it does change through the years.'

Allison Josefsen's family are spread across fishing communities on the East Coast as far as North Shields.

'I've lost contact with all the old fishing people up north. I mean I haven't been back up, but my daughter she's a Geordie so she goes and stays with her dad quite a bit. It used to be lovely at North Shields to walk round the fish quay and it's dead, there's nothing there no more. There's no boats or anything.

'If it wasn't for the Fishermen's Mission and the chapel, the fishermen'd just be forgot about now. They really would. It's a shame. With the miners they have mining colonies up north, there's a big place you can go in. Whereas... you've got something now at Hartlepool, you've got a discovery centre and then you've got this one here. But you think about how many fishing ports there is, from one end of this country to Scotland. But I think fishermen have just faded out now.

'All of the fishermen now are on these standby boats and survey boats 'cos there's no fishing boats left. I blame Thatcher for all that. Shipyards, I mean when I first married, on a dinnertime you couldn't go out your house – there was a thousand men walking up the bank. Now there's nothing, it's just dead.'

Like many former trawlermen, Annie Bell's husband suffered from emphysema – a work-related illness. By the time he approached his union for support, the ships and their owners had long gone.

'He took emphysema, and that was from working on the old ships after the war, down below in the engine room. Of course, fishermen didn't know them days that you could claim for illnesses such as that. It's only this last ten years that it's all come out, 'cos a lot of them did die with that emphysema, you know, it was called bad chest, bronchitis or anything like that. Then when he took bad a few year ago, they x-rayed him and asked him where he'd worked and all that, and told him he'd got emphysema of the lungs.

'I don't know who it was, some bloke on a committee somewhere, engineering committee or something, looked into it and found out it was all this lagging on board the ships, but by then all the ships had been sold and the owners was living abroad or somewhere else so there was nobody to claim off.

'The engineers' union people was very good, they did their best for all of them, but the ships were sold, broke up, and the owners, they're not responsible now because they're already sold out. I mean one big firm, they said the owners went and bought a golf course abroad somewhere. Well, it would cost thousands to trace them and take it to court...as the union said, *you couldn't do it, and we haven't got the money, nobody's got the money*. The firms stabbed a lot of the fishermen in the back, I mean really stabbed them in the back. They was good men, they could have kept some ships, I mean because they was up and coming young men that was gonna follow their fathers' footsteps. If they'd give them a chance, then they'd have had a fishing fleet again. It was just greed, pure greed, because the government offered them money to scrap the ships and the money was there so they took it and the fishermen, "Oh it doesn't matter about you, you'll get a job somewhere; you can go on the dole."'

16. DOLLY HARDIE AND THE FIGHT FOR COMPENSATION

'...fishermen obviously wanted to campaign, but didn't know where to start.'

In the fight for compensation, Grimsby found its most ardent advocate in Dolly Hardie. In the course of researching The Women They Left Behind, we contacted Dolly in the summer and autumn of 2008. Each time it was clear that in spite of her support for the book and the desire to tell her own story, she was not well enough to be interviewed. Although by no means alone in the struggle to secure a fair deal for fishermen, she became identified as the campaign's figurehead. Her indomitable spirit and determination, forged by years as the daughter, wife and mother of fishermen, made her an extraordinary campaigner.

Born into a fishing family in Grimsby's Harrington Street in 1920, Dolly Hardie experienced how perilous a life at sea could be when her father was killed in a U-boat attack on his trawler, the *Wigmore,* in November 1939. By then she had met and married fisherman Bill Hardie. Bill was called up for service with the Royal Navy and like many women during the war, Dolly served as a driver. When Bill came home in 1946, they bought their first home together and Bill returned to fishing.

Eventually becoming a skipper, like many of his counterparts Bill would take his wife out to sea on pleasure trips. On one occasion they ran into trouble, but Dolly kept calm. Her daughter Jayne recalls:

'The bridge was all smashed in, but my dad said she wasn't frightened. He said, "Your mum was on my bunk with water all around her, the bridge had fetched the water in, and she was eating a sandwich and asked me to carry her to the toilet because she wasn't going to get her feet wet."'

With her roots in the fishing industry, Dolly had always been concerned about the welfare of fishermen and their families. Her sisters were married to fishermen and Dolly was the first port of call if they had worries or needed advice. This support extended to other fishermen's wives. Many women who faced problems when their husbands were away at sea went to Dolly for advice, and she did her best to help.

When the industry declined and distant-water fishermen found themselves unemployed, Dolly's concern for those involved became public knowledge. Like most Grimbarians of her generation, Dolly believed that fishing was an important part of Grimsby's heritage and she was determined to secure financial support for those in need. At a time when wholesale decline was beginning to impact on British industry and workers were laid off, paid off or re-trained, fishermen were classed as casual labour with no rights to redundancy payments.

Josephine Gibney, herself the wife of a deep-water trawlerman, worked closely with Dolly over many years and was instrumental in giving the campaign much-needed early momentum.

'When the ships first started tying up, me husband was sat here and I got the paper -his bag was packed upstairs to go to sea - and I said, "You won't be going to sea anymore." He said, *why?* It was on the front of the paper, the ships all tied up. They never even had the decency to tell them. He never did go to sea again. I started by writing to viewpoint about it and Dolly came to see me. She said, "We've had meetings at the pub, we should get together." And that's how we got started. I didn't know Dolly until then 'cos her husband was a skipper.

'We sold things, ran race nights and that at Cleethorpes. We tried everything. We went to London. That just about knocked me out. I don't know about politics, but they went in this big room and there was dozens of people there and different MPs and they was trying to say about how much the fishermen should get. And I wanted to try and get into the meeting and this MP started pushing and shoving me saying, "You're not going in."'

In 1978, Dolly wrote to request redundancy payments for her husband and son. The court rejected the request, but this simple act of letter writing was in itself an initial lesson for the novice campaigner. As daughter Jayne remembers:

> 'Of course the reply came back saying they weren't entitled to redundancy. But sending the letter that meant that my father and my brother weren't statute barred, so then my mum fought the case; they weren't barred because they'd sent that letter.'

Soon Dolly found herself fighting for the thousands of other fishermen in different ports.

> 'The fishermen obviously wanted to campaign, but didn't know where to start and mum was very good at putting a letter together and that evolved into thousands of letters. She was also very good at getting people to do things for her, like she would coerce me into typing up letters. She got a committee together, and they went over to meet some others in Hull, and then that also expanded to Fleetwood, and she got to know a lot of people across the country, and actually went across to Fleetwood and Hull to make speeches. They started the British Fishermen's Association with the help of Austin Mitchell.'

Austin Mitchell remembers an early visit to the House of Commons and his first meeting with Dolly.

> 'It must have been about 1982 they formed the British Fishermen's Association at a pub on Grimsby Road in Cleethorpes, I think it was *Darley's*. They came down to London to lobby ministers. I think Bunny Newton, a famous skipper and club owner, - he made a lot of money out of fishing - and he paid for a bus to bring them down to London, by the time they arrived some of them were fairly drunk. The Tory Government was in at the time, and I met them, and I think that was when I first met Dolly. After that she began to come regularly to surgery and take up the compensation issue.'

The intervention of Humberside Law Centre solicitor Humphrey Forrest in taking on the cases of six Hull fishermen was a major step forward for the campaign. Before Forrest, no commercial lawyer had been prepared to risk backing the fishermen's cause. Dolly provided evidence for the case in which Forrest argued that the fishermen in question were employed, rather than casual workers, and that the nature of the industry meant they had been totally dependent on their employers.

Forrest argued the case at tribunal in Hull and won, only for the Government to argue that fishermen were not eligible for redundancy payments because they had not applied for them. Lawyers and local MPs argued that fishermen had not applied because they had been advised by the Department for Trade and Industry that they were not entitled to payment.

In communities where word of mouth was the main means of communication, proof that fishermen had been wrongly advised was unlikely to be documented. Undeterred, Dolly contacted the fishermen's employment office on the docks and received confirmation; the men *had* been told that, as casual workers, they were not entitled to apply for redundancy payments. They had been misadvised.

In 1993, following a decision by the Court of Appeal, Employment Minister Ann Widdecombe finally agreed to *ex gratia* payments as a result of the evidence provided by Dolly on behalf of the British Fisherman's Association. However, the payments would only be made to former distant-water trawlermen who could prove that, at the time of their redundancy, they met the qualifying requirements for statutory redundancy; that being, they could demonstrate two years continuous service with a single employer.

This failed to take into consideration the working practices of the industry where employment patterns often required fishermen to move between employers. The scheme operated by ship owners and the Employment Department to ensure adequate numbers of trawlermen were available for work meant that fishermen were compelled to cover vacancies on the trawlers of whichever company needed men, or lose their benefits. The supposed breaks in employment that the 'pool system' encouraged were more common in Grimsby than in any other port. Men with 35 years service received only a few hundred pounds in compensation.

In a 1995 letter to Austin Mitchell responding to Tony Baldry, the new Minister of State for MAFF, Dolly's message is characteristically direct:

> 'I assure the Minister the trawler owners of the Humber have no honour and do not know the meaning of the word and they did exactly nothing for Grimsby, Hull and Fleetwood, so there must be a question of "missing money in the normal sense of the term."'

In the following year, Dolly Hardie was awarded the MBE. After the investiture, when asked what had been said, Dolly replied that the Queen commented how unusual it was for a woman to receive an award for fishing.

Dolly addressing fishermen at the Ice House, Grimsby

Messages of congratulation on the award give some indication of the affection and respect the 'skipper's wife from Grimsby' had earned. Dolly received letters from Fisheries Minister William Waldegrave and The Royal Naval Patrol Service. She was also formally recognised with an award from the Law Society for her involvement in highlighting the inaccuracies of the compensation system; all the more remarkable as she'd had no legal training.

The campaign intensified with the election of the New Labour Government in 1997. John Prescott, the new Deputy Prime Minister was one of several influential MPs with their constituency base in the Humber region. In November that year the new DTI Minister met with a delegation of MPs from the ports around Britain's coast most affected by the redundancies. In March 1998, MPs signed a letter criticising the existing *ex gratia* scheme for being at odds with the 'pool system'.

When Hull MP Alan Johnson spoke in the House of Commons on 8 March 1999, he gave a damning indictment of the way fishermen had been treated.

> 'Promises were made and they were nothing less than the men concerned deserved. They were courageous; they went out in the most difficult conditions, and distant water fishing was the most dangerous of occupations. They worked in Arctic conditions beyond the north-cape bank, and the mortality rate was 14 times that for coal mining.'

The debate laid bare the injustice suffered by trawlermen whose livelihoods were taken without compensation. Johnson set out the conditions of the original payments made to trawler owners:

> 'Compensation was paid by the Ministry of Agriculture, Fisheries and Food (MAFF) to trawler owners to decommission their ships. More than £100 million was paid to trawler owners—not one penny of which went to the men. That is very important, because the criteria under which that money was paid was made absolutely clear in a letter on 12 March 1996 from MAFF to another supporter of the campaign, the former Prime Minister, the right hon. Member for Old Bexley and Sidcup (Sir E. Heath). MAFF said: Both Labour and Conservative Governments offered compensation to vessel owners to alleviate the position that the industry found itself in through the loss of these fishing grounds following the imposition of the 200 mile limit. The vessel owners, in particular, found themselves with considerable assets that could no longer be used. The trawlermen had considerable assets that could no longer be used, too: their skill, energy and courage... millions of pounds were paid to trawler owners, but not a penny was paid in compensation to the trawlermen, despite the promises that were made.'

Continuing the debate, Joan Humble, MP for Fleetwood highlighted the role of women in her own constituency:

> '... It is important to remember the role that women had, and still have, in fishing communities such as Fleetwood—wives and mothers, they were left behind for weeks at a time to raise children, look after the home, pay the bills and wait in the hope that their husbands would return safely from one of the most dangerous jobs in the world. We are talking about whole communities and about families, not just about the men who went out on the boats.'

As a campaigner, Dolly realised the value in publicity, and found willing support for the campaign from the local media. In July 2000, the *Grimsby Telegraph* ran the campaign *The Heart of the Community* aimed at ensuring MPs kept up pressure on the seemingly interminable bureaucratic process.

Finally, in 2000 The Department for Business, Enterprise and Regulatory Reform (formerly the Department of Trade and Industry) announced a scheme to compensate former UK-based Icelandic water trawlermen who had lost their jobs as a consequence of the settlement of the final cod war and the subsequent collapse of the fishing industry.

Sadly Bill Hardie died in 2001, after more than 60 years of marriage. Jayne remembers how the campaign had taken over her parents' lives.

> 'I think sometimes it drove my father absolutely mad, because she was obsessed by it. Every conversation you'd have would start off with what *you* were talking about and finish off with something to do with the compensation case. So as he retired - he didn't retire until he was nearly seventy - he was happy for her to do it, but it took over their lives really; they had filing cabinets full of stuff in the spare bedroom, mum was always on the phone and people was always ringing her, so it wasn't very peaceful for them, but he was supportive. He was the President of the Royal Naval Patrol Service so he had his own things going on, so it wasn't just all about mum.'

Dolly and Bill Hardie

In March 2004, trawlers fishing around the Faroe Islands were included in the compensation scheme, adding a further 21 vessels to the qualifying list. The issue of qualifying vessels wasn't without problems. When the scheme launched, the government requested the Hull branch of the British Fishermen's Association to provide a list of trawlers meeting its qualifying criteria, i.e. those it believed had operated in Icelandic waters. The list's omissions and government's failure to consult with members of all ports led to contention in Grimsby and fuelled the fight for fair compensation.

Government's refusal to accept that men were told they had to work in the North Sea if they could not fish in Iceland led Austin Mitchell to take evidence to the

Ombudsman, who after an investigation, agreed that fishermen were indeed forced to take employment. In her report, the Ombudsman ruled in the trawlermen's favour and made three findings: firstly, that the scheme was devised and launched before it was appropriate to do so; secondly, that there was a mismatch between what the scheme was intended to deliver and what it was capable of delivering; and finally, that the problems identified during the operation of the scheme should have led to a comprehensive review.

In April 2008, the government began a further investigation of the Ombudsman's findings; this involved a further examination of the scheme's eligibility criteria including the list of eligible vessels. It was expected that the process would take four or five months. Austin Mitchell and Shona McIsaac met with Business and Enterprise Minister Pat Mcfadden to express their concern at the delay in paying compensation. The process was optimistically expected to take three months. The delay yet again undermined the hard work of campaigners committed to ensuring a basic level of fair compensation.

Dolly continued campaigning and was involved on the committee that helped Grimsby commemorate its fishermen in the form of a memorial in St James' Square. In November 2008, Dolly Hardie died at the age of 88 after a long illness.

She had been a regular visitor to Austin Mitchell's MP's surgeries for 26 years. Working alongside her, he witnessed the qualities she brought to the campaign.

> 'A lot of the fishermen were frightened of her, but a lot loved her. She could never relax and say *it's all over, we've won*; she always pushed it further. They backed her. She used to come to my surgery every fortnight to keep up the pressure. She was tough. She was consistent. She kept pushing, and she knew more about fishing than any of the ministers she was dealing with. She kept all their letters so she was the source of a lot of information. She received a lot of correspondence from the owners and from fishermen, and from the government saying why it wasn't possible. I mean at first she thought it was easy, all you've got to do is be right and they'll give way, but it doesn't work like that.'

In later life, Dolly's influence and involvement as a community leader had become sought after for a variety of issues. Jayne remembers:

> 'She worked really hard to move forward. As she got older the things she sorted out were not just about compensation; it might be the widow of somebody who was financially in trouble and she'd go to the different charities and see what she could sort out.'

The tributes to Dolly Hardie were as widespread and as heartfelt as the people whose lives she had touched. At the annual fisheries debate in Parliament on 20 November, MPs remembered Dolly, with Shona McIsaac concluding she had been, '... one of the best fighters for fishermen in this country.' And that, '... our community will truly miss her.' The message of condolence from the fishermen of Fleetwood thanked Dolly Hardie, *who fought for Grimsby but never left Fleetwood out,* and who made sure that the fishermen of Fleetwood were included when compensation was paid in 1993 and 2000.

A month after Dolly's death, in December 2008, the Government's original compensation scheme was finally deemed unfair and a new scheme put in place making payments based on each trawlerman's total service on vessels that fished in Icelandic waters. This means that the impact of any breaks from the industry will be sharply reduced and will enable more than a thousand trawlermen around the country to have their cases reviewed. One suspects that this is the legacy Dolly would appreciate most.

Dolly Hardie with Austin Mitchell MP

The decline of the fishing industry had enormous impact on Grimsby's economic and social well-being that no amount of subsequent compensation could tackle. The loss to the local economy of high-earning skippers and owners; rising unemployment among former fishermen and those whose jobs had depended on the industry, all added to feelings that Grimsby and the fishing industry had been dealt an unfair hand. While it is true that some fishermen took their skills abroad, others stayed to fight for compensation. Many died without receiving a penny.

The worst effects of decline came in those areas where fishing money had traditionally been spent. Freeman Street's vibrancy has been replaced by empty shop units and boarded pubs; pockets of deprivation have become rooted in former fishing communities. Regeneration funding has provided little more than a sticking plaster for the loss of the industry on which the town was built. To date, attempts at renaissance and re-building have struggled to deliver real progress.

The Women They Left Behind offers a snapshot of good times enjoyed and hardships endured by Grimsby's fishing communities. The women who supported the industry were resilient and inspirational, and their stories are a fitting tribute to a proud fishing heritage.

A SHANTY IN OLD SHANTY TOWN

Joe Young, John Siras, and Little Jack Little

I'm up in the world,
but I'd give the world to be where I used to be,
A heavenly nest
where I rest the best,
means more than the world to me.

It's only a shanty
in old Shanty Town,
the roof is so slanty it touches the ground.
But my tumbled down shack by an old railroad track,
like a millionaire's mansion is calling me back.

I'd give up a palace if I were a king.
It's more than a palace, it's my everything.
There's a queen waiting there with a silvery crown
in a shanty in old Shanty Town.

ABOUT THE AUTHORS

Nick Triplow

Nick is a freelance writer and editor. Born in London in 1964, Nick studied writing, publishing and English at Middlesex University and was awarded a distinction on Sheffield Hallam University's MA Writing course in 2007. As Programme Manager of North East Lincolnshire's Single Regeneration Budget Scheme, he was given an insight to the way former fishing communities had dealt with the decline of the industry. He was instrumental in instigating a range of community-based regeneration projects including the Community Press Office - now CPO Media.

Nick is the author of *Family Ties – Stories from Hall's Barton Ropery* and editor of *Article* – Northern Lincolnshire's monthly independent guide to the arts. He has recently co-written the script for *Ted's Return Home,* a short film about Ted Lewis, the crime writer and author of *Get Carter*. He is currently writing a biography of Lewis and completing his second novel.

Tina Bramhill

27 year old Tina has a passion for writing and design and worked in community media prior to *The Women They Left Behind*. She graduated with a first class honours degree in Professional Writing in 2008, during which she became fascinated with books that use historical events and settings as a basis for drama and fiction. It was this interest which drew her to the project.

She has recently published a number of pieces of short fiction and is currently developing a radio drama based on the lives of women in the fishing industry.

'This project has given me a real insight to my home town and made me realise that there are so many stories out there that haven't been told.'

Jade Shepherd

Grimsby born Jade studied History at Lancaster University from 2004 – 2007. Staying on to complete an MA in Historical Research, Jade graduated in December 2008. She is planning to begin her PhD in September at Queen Mary College, University of London.

Jade's academic interests include: the history of medicine and psychiatry, sexuality, and gender, particularly how attitudes towards gender change and differ in different societies and industries.

'The project highlights the experience and role of women in Grimsby's fishing industry, something not previously considered. It shows how important women's roles were and it demonstrates the struggles they faced.'

About CPO Media

CPO Media evolved from a social regeneration organisation which formed in 2002 named the Community Press Office.

The Community Press Office's role for the first six years of its existence was to produce micro-local media in areas that had high levels of deprivation – largely as a result of the decline of the fishing industry. Within the eight titles published at this time, history articles penned by local volunteers often related tales of Grimsby's trawler town which were extremely popular with readers. It was a story that they felt had to be told. It was this enthusiasm and a hidden archive of material which was the genesis for *The Women They Left Behind.*

As the Community Press Office metamorphasised into CPO Media we have not forgotten how important the town's heritage is to our readers. We continue to support regeneration, and new generations in the continuing task of re-identifying an area whose soul was taken away. Many of the stories told in these pages are testament to the wonderful women who supported an industry and helped to create the heritage written here.

Stephen Ryder, Managing Director, CPO Media

ACKNOWLEDGEMENTS

The Authors would like to thank: Heritage Lottery Fund, without whose support *The Women They Left Behind* would have remained an unfulfilled vision; CPO Media and the staff, particularly Stephen Ryder for project management and proof reading and Gillian Kapka for press-passing; Focus 7 for loan of the Lydia Sinclair interview; the *Grimsby Telegraph* for their support and the use of their photographic archives (special thanks to Linda Roberts and Steve Richards); The Royal National Mission to Deep Sea Fishermen (Grimsby); Grimsby Central Library; Fishing Heritage Centre (special thanks to Mark Tindle and Esther Farrow); Imperial War Museum; National Archives; British Library and The Modern Records Centre, Warwick. The 'QUALITY STREET®' name and image is reproduced with the kind permission of Société des Produits Nestlé S.A.

We are grateful to the following CPO Media volunteers who helped with interviews and transcription: Tony Kyle, Katharine Sinderson, Andrew Taylor and Jim White

Most importantly, thanks to those who gave their time and memories to us freely and openly:

Jayne Bacon
Annie Bell
Rose Blake
Merle Boyington
Emma Brennan
Derek Brown
Mike Connor
Janet Cox
Graham Dolby
Olga Drever
Deslys Fairfield
Josephine Gibney & son Russell
Ann Graves
Joan Harrison
Maureen Harvey
Peter Hickson

Mary-Rose Jessop
Allison Josefsen
Marjorie Louis & daughter Lorraine
Angela McMullen
Austin Mitchell MP
Margaret Monger
Sheila Ottley
Beverley Read
Margaret Robinson
Lydia Sinclair
Elizabeth Stark
Jean Teasdale
Doreen Tyson
Mary Jane Walmsley
Rita Whittle
Sally Wilbourne
Peter Woods
Dawn Wraith

Thanks to you all, without your help and input this book would not have been possible.

BIBLIOGRAPHY

Barker, E.J, & Crum, J.P, *Grimsby Trawlers*, Oxford: Oxford University Press, 1961

Bell, J. J, *British Trawlers in Wartime*, London: Readers Library Publishing Co: London, 1939

Boswell, D, *The History of Grimsby's Fishing Industry*, Grimsby Borough Publishing, 1976

Chapman, P, *Grimsby: The Story of the World's Greatest Fishing Port*, Derby: Breedon Books Publishing, 2007

Cox, C. B, *The Sailing Trawlers and Liners of Grimsby*

Dowling, A, *Grimsby: Making the Town, 1800 – 1914*

Drury, E, *The Great Grimsby Story: 1850-1993*

Ekberg, C, *Grimsby Fish: the story of the port and the decline and fall of the deep-water industry*, Buckingham: Barraduca, 1984

Elliot, P, *Allied Minesweeping in World War Two*, Cambridge: Stephans, 1979

French, C, *The Role of the Fishing Industry in the Development of Grimsby*

Gilchrist, A, *Cod Wars and How to Lose Them*, Edinburgh Press, 1978

Gillet, E, *A History of Grimsby*, Hull University Press, 1970

Goddard, J & Spalding, R, *Fish 'n' Ships: the rise and fall of Grimsby – the world's premier fishing port*, Clapham, Lancaster: Dalesman Books, 1987

Hammond, R.J, *Official History of the Second World War*, Vol II, Civil Series, 1956

Hardy, C, *Grimsby at War*, Runcorn: Archive Publications, 1989

Hardy, H, *A Minesweepers Victory...A Silent Service of the Royal Navy*, Weybridge: Keydex, 1979

Hart, J, *The Anglo-Icelandic Cod War of 1972-3: a case study of a fishery dispute*, University of California, Berkeley, 1976

Hart, M, 'Religion in Cleethorpes', *Grimsby Evening Telegraph*, September 11 1993

Holroyd, J, *The Great Grimsby Lock Out of 1901*, Harprint & Co Ltd, 1986

Hough, R, *The Great War at Sea 1914-1918*, 2nd edn. Birlinn, 2001

Hutson, H. C, *Grimsby's Fighting Fleet: Trawlers and U-boats during the Second World War*, Hutton Press

Jackson, G, *Grimsby and the Haven Company 1796-1846*

Jeffreys, K, *Anthony Crosland*, Cohen, 1999

Johannesson, G. T, *Troubled Waters: Cod War, Fishing Disputes, and Britain's Fight*

for the Freedom of the High Seas, 1948-1964, North Atlantic Fisheries History Association, 2007
Jonsson, H, *Friends in Conflict: The Anglo-Icelandic Cod Wars and the Law of the Sea,* London: C Hurst & Company, 1982
Lincoln, B, *The Rise of Grimsby,* Hull University Press, 1970
Losses of H.M. Ships and Auxiliaries During the War 1914 to 1918, London: By his Majesty's Stationary Office, 1919
Lund, P & Ludlam, H, *Out Sweeps!: the Story of the minesweepers in World War Two,* London: New English Library, 1979
Manley, D, "There's Something Wrong With Our Bloody Fish Today" Wargaming the "Cod Wars"
Melvin, J, *Minesweeper: the Motor Minesweeper in World War Two,* Worcester: Square One, 1992
Peasgood, D, *Grimsby: A History & Celebration,* Frith Bank Company Ltd, 2004
Put Together in Haste: 'Cod Wars' Trawlermen's Compensation Scheme, 2nd Report, session 2006-7, 21 Feb 2007
Roberts, R. F, *Trawlers of Humberside,* Tempus Publishing Limited, 2005
Robinson, R, *Trawling: The Rise and Fall of the British Trawl Industry,* University of Exeter Press, 1996
Thompson, *The Hull and Grimsby Stern Trawling Fleet 1961-1988,* Beverly: Hutton Press, 1988
Thor, J, *British Trawlers and Iceland,* 1995
Thor, J & Utgafa, F, *British Trawlers in Icelandic Waters,* 1992
Toghill, G, *Royal Navy Trawlers* Part 2 Requisitioned Trawlers
Walker, D. M, *The Labour Mightily: a tale of inshore fishing in war and peace,* A. Brown, 1947
Weekes, A, *Minesweeping Operations – North Sea and Normandy Coast,* issue 14, 1998
Welch, A, *The Royal Navy in the Cod Wars: Britain and Iceland in Conflict, 1958-1961, 1972-1973, 1975-76,* Liskeard: Maritime Books, 2006

Newspapers and magazines

Bygones
Fishing Gazette
Fishing News
Grimsby Telegraph

The Times
'Great Britain in War-Time: XIV – The Humber Ports: Shipwrecked Crews at Grimsby, *Times*, February 22 1940
His Majesty's Minesweepers, 1943 prepared for the Admiralty by the Ministry of Information
Manual of Minesweeping, 1940
Letters/memos from a Confidential M. O. D folder regarding Britain's position after the end of the cod wars.
Conversion of Merchant Ships into Armed Merchant Cruisers, 1939
Announcements by the British Government, Reykjavik, 25 November 1975
Prime Ministers Office, Reykjavik, Press Release, 8 January 1976

Websites

http://www.mcdoa.org.uk/MCD_History_Frames.htm
'Russian Claimed he Killed 'Buster' Crabb, the Frogman who inspired James Bond', *Times Online,* November 16 2007
'Details on Vanished 'spy' Diver', http://news.bbc.co.uk/1/hi/uk/6089952.stm
'Russian 'killed UK diver' in 1956', http://news.bbc.co.uk/1/hi/uk/7097646.stm
http://news.bbc.co.uk/onthisday/hi/dates/stories/may/9/newsid_4741000/4741060.stm
http://www.royalnavalmuseum.org/CuratorsChoiceofBusterCrabbmedalsJune2006.htm
Hansard

Videos – kindly loaned by Pete Woods & Peter Hickson

The Cod Wars - BBC Documentary
Fish & Ships
Trawler Town